Unmuted

Leaders Discover Their Voice to Speak Up and Stand Out

A Lead from Within Anthology

Inner Circle Press

Unmuted – Leaders Discover their Voice to Speak Up and Stand Out

A Lead From Within Anthology by

Kim Kleeman

Joy Poli

Becca Berkenstadt

Natalia Duarte

Angela Kesting

Christene Lankford-Grow

Simona Pappalardo

Michelle Valiukenas

Every effort has been made to ensure this book is free from errors or omissions. The information and advice contained in this book are based upon the research and the personal and professional experiences of the authors. Some names and characteristics have been changed, some events have been compressed, and some dialogue has been recreated. Chapters reflect the authors' present recollections of experiences over time. The opinions herein are of each individual contributor. All writings are the property of individual contributors.

The publisher, editor, and authors are not responsible for any adverse effects or consequences resulting from the use of any of the suggestions, preparations, procedures discussed in this book.

Publisher: Inner Circle Press

Ebook ISBN: 979-8-9946624-0-3

Paperback ISBN: 979-8-9946624-1-0

Cover Design: Danielle Epperson and Miblart Cover Designs

Book Coach: Tami Palmer

Editor and Formatter: Alina Rubin, Hearts and Sails Author Services

Proofreader: Wm. (Bill) Bullion

Marketing Strategist: Becca Berkenstadt, Wordly Strategies

Table of Contents

The Inner Circle Press Takes Lead From Within from Idea to Series

Kim Kleeman and Joy Poli

As the Inner Circle enters its 9th year, and the **Inner Circle Press** debuts its 2nd *Lead From Within* anthology, we are proud to stand alongside another wonderful group of leaders who have taken the time to share their stories.

When we published the first *Lead From Within* anthology, we stepped into the process with curiosity and hope. We believed deeply in the power of storytelling and leadership, but we didn't fully know where the journey would lead. What unfolded was something truly special. In the first book, we needed entrepreneurs who share their proven traits for success. And they did! Thank you for your wise words and for paving the way for future members to be able to become part of this wonderful legacy.

This second group of authors continues that legacy with *Unmuted*. They're sharing their own stories, and what wonderful journeys they are! Each contributor in this anthology has chosen to use their voice—to reflect on the moments, people, and experiences that have shaped who they are as leaders and as individuals. Some have tragic moments, or insightful conversations, or others have taken their cues from the people (and even fur-babies) who love them.

Each story in this book shares how important people and events have shaped their lives. The process of writing this book created an opportunity for each one to use their voice in a way that made sense for them and give them the ability to share great lessons for the reader to take away.

Take time to read each chapter, and feel free to reach out to the author on their LinkedIn page or website. They would love to hear from you and how their story impacted you. Perhaps they are the next speaker for your group, or consultant for your business. We know we have recommended each and every one of them.

This is a memorable selection of stories that will inspire you too to find your voice and speak up when it counts! Every voice has the power to make a difference when it is shared with courage and intention.

The *Lead From Within* series, including this book, promotes using your voice for the greater good. Let's speak up and make the world a better place.

Better Together,

Kim Kleeman and Joy Poli

Prologue by the Founders

Kim Kleeman and Joy Poli

Leading with Openness: The Power of Vulnerability

As co-founders we established the Inner Circle Business Network (oinnero.com) on a foundation of shared core principles almost ten years ago. Our goals are to develop leaders, promote people we genuinely enjoy working with, connect them forward, and, crucially, cultivate a community where people would want to stick around and deepen their relationships. Most of these values mirror the ones leaders have honed over years of striving to be a good friend, a good partner, and an impactful citizen—all roles that matter deeply to us. However, the real work lies in maintaining the vulnerability required to remain open to ideas, different styles of leadership and ways of doing things that are unlike your own. Practicing adaptability and flexibility is what allows you to sustain this openness as you move through the world.

We believe it's imperative to find ways to show up, speak up, and use your voice to move the needle in the direction of the thing you care about—whether that's helping others, making the world a better place, or simply loving those that are closest to you around you. Our true voice is clear, loud, opinionated, confident, and friendly—most of the time. *What's yours?* It's important to us that people feel included and that they shine and reach their best potential. *How are you building up your confidence and voice?*

Here are 4 insights for leaders who want to step up, speak up, and find their voice:

Shape the Path to Be the Leader You'd Like to Become Someday

What do you want in life? When coaching leaders (or aspiring leaders), we ask them to articulate what their vision is and make sure the dream we build and plan for matches their daily life. It's hard to make goals if they aren't clear on their purpose and the life they want to live. Once you know the type of leader you want to be (or if NOTHING else, think about the type of leader you DON'T want to be and pick the opposite) then you can start to actively strive to become it.

Yep, pick up that imposter syndrome and turn it upside down by full-on accepting that you are being an imposter at first. And as you grow into the leader you want to be one day, you'll look back and realize through micro-steps, experiences, decisions in crisis moments, and the path the universe wants you to take—got you there. *What could you decide to do today that gets you closer to your BEST life?*

Leadership Leveling Up Is Personal

We all have things we don't particularly like about ourselves. At each stage of life, there have been times we needed to be a better version of ourselves—a kinder, gentler, more patient version. In fact, many people needed a reminder that we all carry burdens. Members in the Inner Circle needed us to give them some grace. Perhaps, health became the focus, or for another, friendship became the missing factor and they needed to grow it back. Perhaps a member had made some bad decisions and needed to try again in a safe space. These growth opportunities are a way to test your leadership skills. *What elements of your ideal day are missing? How can you start to bring that back into your life?*

Many members join us at a time of transition, whether it's a new job, role, or path. It's our goal to help them live their best life. This takes some introspection and some dedication to improving yourself a little bit at a time over time, consistently.

Becoming the best version of yourself takes some work. Note: If you have young kids, that work might have to be a slower path than others. Enjoy the moments and try to move forward and don't lose sight of what you're doing it for. Of course, much of the time you may have never felt that you were doing anything (or everything) all too well. That's ok! All is not lost! If you are someone who has the time, you can plan a framework for how you can build your best life as well. It won't always go that way but when you have time to focus on that path, you can take dedicated actionable steps towards the life you want to live. *How can you take time to work on yourself in some impactful way? What impact do you want to have on others?*

Unmuting: Finding Your Voice

For people like us—a mother, a wife, a daughter, and sister—these leadership traits show up taking care of those who we love, and those who are our team—partners and allies. We shine when part of a team, and our leadership is activated by that. Stepping forward and speaking up is important for ourselves and our members.

As coaches, we give activities to our clients in finding their voice. Whether you call it "taking up space," "being too much," or "finding your voice," the goal is for you to become comfortable with your style, tone, and way of saying things. That means listening to your inner dialogue and implementing the good stuff into writing, speaking, images, video, or other creative endeavors. Each author in this book has done so and we are so proud to know them and watch them continue to shine.

Once you've found your voice, utilizing it in the proper context is the next big step. It's hard to step up and speak up, but if *you* don't, then who will? Things often go awry or fall apart without a leader. Someone who is willing to take the risk and step forward to coalesce the group to reach the mission. Whether that's putting on a play, a work project, or helping a neighbor, a leader is needed. *How can you find your voice and speak up?*

Finding your voice and sharing it with others is key to leadership. That's why speech/communications class is mandatory for high school and college students. **Finding your voice and knowing how to create your own original thoughts are integral to aligning yourself with your strengths and the path you can have the most impact on.** *Wouldn't that be amazing? To truly have a positive impact in a field or industry you care about?*

Well, keep taking those baby steps toward it and you can for sure make some impact. Unless that space isn't for you, then leave it and create the space that's best for you—it's likely needed and others will come too. Becoming a community builder means you'll never be alone and you can help others feel the same. Just know that it will take time and selfless dedication.

When Leading Is Lonely And When It's Worth It

The authors in this book are leaders who live these leadership traits of speaking up, showing up, and they all share ways that they have found their voice in their own chapters. We are so lucky to know them, lead alongside them and have seen many of them grow into amazing CEOs, consultants, coaches, and more!

They have done this in many ways. Some unmuted themselves and stood up, some made sure to stand out, some listened to their intuition and stepped into their destiny, and some were brave enough to take a risk and leap into a new world, leaving the old one behind. It's amazing to think each author's journey is rooted in experience and courage to be someone they desired to be. And now we are even more inspired to step further into our leadership era. *Are you ready, too?*

Kim Kleeman

Kim Kleeman builds businesses and brands. She is the founder of Accelerate Successfully, CEO of the **100-year-old family commercial bakery Simon Bros Bakery**, and co-founder of the **Professional Moms Community Network**, which connects more than **12,000 women across multiple chapters**. She also co-founded the **Inner Circle Business Network** and **Inner Circle Press** with her sister Joy Poli. Kim is the author of *Lead From Within*, a **Global Literary Award winner**, and curates collaborative leadership anthologies featuring entrepreneurs and community leaders.

Connect with Kim

Accelerate Successfully acceleratesuccessfully.com

Simon Brothers Bakery and Labs simonbroslabs.com

Professional Moms Community Network

professionalmomscommunitynetwork.com

Inner Circle oinnero.com

LinkedIn www.linkedin.com/in/acceleratesuccessfully

Joy Poli

Joy Poli is a master networker, relationship builder, and leadership connector who helps professionals elevate their influence and build powerful communities. As **Networking Coach for Accelerate Successfully**, Joy equips clients with the tools and mindset needed to create high-value, strategic relationships that fuel growth, opportunity, and long-term success.

Joy is also the **Co-Founder of The Inner Circle Network**, an exclusive professional community focused on business development, sales mastery, and leadership excellence. Through curated connections, dynamic training, and thought leadership platforms, Joy empowers members to grow their visibility and bottom line through authentic collaboration.

A true advocate for community-based leadership, Joy serves as **Chapter Leader of the Glenview/Northbrook Professional Moms**—a branch of the Professional Moms Community Network—supporting over 2,500 women balancing careers and family.

She leads both online and in-person gatherings, cultivating connection, mentorship, and support for professional moms at every stage.

In addition to her coaching and community-building roles, Joy is the **Owner of Strategic Talent Resources**, where she offers strategic HR advisory and recruiting solutions tailored to each business's unique needs. As a trusted **PEO Alternative**, Joy and her team help companies attract, hire, and retain top talent with a customized, hands-on approach.

Joy has fused her passions and professional expertise into one mission: helping others connect forward with clarity, purpose, and intention. Whether she's guiding clients through strategic networking or supporting business leaders with talent strategy, Joy brings heart, wisdom, and results to every relationship.

Connect with Joy

Accelerate Successfully

acceleratesuccessfully.com/coaching/network-coaching

Inner Circle oinnero.com

Strategic Talent Resources strategictalentresources.com

LinkedIn https://www.linkedin.com/in/joypoli

More Than They Expected

Christene Lankford-Grow

I never thought I would be sitting down to write about leadership. What I set out to do was make sense of the path I have walked—the moments that shaped me, challenged me, and changed me. The words ahead are not meant to be a lesson in leadership theory. It is a collection of real-life experiences, told through my eyes, in my voice. Some stories will make you laugh; some might make you wince, and others may feel familiar in a way that reminds you of your own journey. These are the stepping stones that led me from being a hard worker with something to prove, to becoming a leader who knows her worth. My hope is that in reading these pages, you will see pieces of your own story—and find clarity, courage, and confidence in your own leadership journey.

If you're a woman chasing leadership, navigating corporate culture, or just trying to figure out how to be bold without burning out—this chapter is for you.

I did not get my seat at the leadership table because someone handed it to me. I earned it—one conversation, one closed deal, one lunch invitation at a time.

Back then, I was in middle management. I showed up, led teams, hit my numbers, and worked a tremendous number of hours. There was a group of men in my office, mostly VPs, who had what I came to think of as "The Guys' Club Lunch." Several times a week, they went out for lunch together, which served as informal strategy discussions. A casual setting where C-suite conversation took place over food and sports talk. The lunches were frequent, so much so that Pad Thai Tuesday became a tagline.

One day, out of nowhere, I got the invite.

I was nervous—not because I did not belong, but because I knew how much it meant. It was not just lunch. It was access. Visibility. A crack in the ceiling. I showed up that day knowing I would need to bring more than just my appetite.

Work talk happened, yes, but so did sports scores, trades, and player stats. And while I already kept up with current events—politics, business, the pulse of the city—I quickly realized I would need to sharpen my sports game. So, I did. I studied. I leaned in on the appropriate conversations and on Sundays I made a habit of knowing the highlights of the sports world and even downloaded a sports app on my phone to keep up with the latest. I made it my business to understand what mattered to the people around that table—not to blend in, but to stand out intelligently.

And then the invitations kept coming.

That's when I understood something I've never forgotten: showing up is the beginning, but staying in the room—and being taken seriously in it—is a different kind of challenge. One that takes awareness, strategy, humility, and mostly courage.

That experience lit a fire in me. It was a defining moment—the beginning of my quiet but powerful rise into senior leadership. Afterward, I advanced to Director and then VP of Sales. I never stopped working hard. I never stopped speaking up. And I never forgot what it felt like to be the only woman at the table—and still hold my own.

That is why I am writing this chapter. Not because I have all the answers, but because I have lived the lessons. I was the one labeled "too much," too much passion and emotion, and the one who kept showing up anyway. I was driven by my passion, a strong will to succeed and an even stronger work ethic.

Work Ethic

For me being in leadership starts with a strong work ethic.

A strong work ethic is not something you are born with, it is something you witness, absorb, and choose to live by. I learned mine by watching my father, who showed me through his actions what it meant to show up, no matter what the circumstance. He was an ironworker who, after a serious fall at an early age, spent the rest of his life walking with a limp. Eventually, the pain became too much to bear, and he underwent surgery that left him in a full body cast for several months. But even then, he did not stop working. A few weeks after his procedure, his cast was removed, and he started using crutches. He requested my mother to purchase a set of workout sweats, extra-large to fit over the remaining cast. His intent was to get up and get back to work. My father returned to his job. He found a way to show up, contribute, and provide for his family—without complaint, without excuse. That image of him, in pain but persevering, is something I carry with me every day.

His example taught me that showing up is not about being at 100%—it is about giving your best with whatever you must give. It is about honoring your commitments, taking pride in your responsibilities, and understanding that the effort you put in reflects not just your abilities but your character. There is quiet dignity in consistent, honest work. It builds trust, it earns respect, and it shapes who you are—not just as a professional, but as a person.

That kind of work ethic creates a ripple effect. When you show up consistently and do your best, it encourages others to rise to that same standard. It strengthens teams, fosters reliability, and builds a culture where people take ownership of their roles. Work ethic is not about grinding—it is about integrity. It is about caring enough to deliver quality, even when no one is watching, and leading by example. I learned that from my father, and it is one of the greatest gifts he could have given me.

Finding Your Voice

But having a strong work ethic was only half the equation. I had to learn to use my voice, especially at the conference table. Early in my career, I often sat in meetings overflowing with energy and ideas but kept them to myself out of fear of being wrong or too bold. I would rehearse responses in my head, waiting for the perfect moment, only to let it pass. Over time, I realized that silence does not serve anyone, not your team, not your organization, and certainly not yourself. Presence isn't just about showing up—it's about staying in the room, engaging in the conversation, and believing that your perspective belongs there just as much as anyone else's.

One of the turning points for me was a boss who not only recognized my potential but also made it a point to draw it out. He had a unique way of redirecting conversations toward me—not to put me on the spot, but to reinforce that I had something valuable to contribute. When a topic came up that aligned with my role or strengths, he would pause the discussion and say, "Let's hear what she thinks." At first, it startled me. But over time, it empowered me. It forced me to be ready, to own my expertise, and to find clarity and confidence in my voice. He did not just open the door for me—he stood behind it and reminded me to walk through.

That experience taught me how crucial it is to have someone in your corner—a champion who sees your strengths before you do and is not afraid to shine a light on them. I was lucky to have a boss who recognized my strengths. Especially as women in leadership, we need more than mentors; we need advocates. People who will not only coach us behind the scenes but will speak our names in rooms of opportunity. That is the power of true leadership, recognizing talent and raising it up. And when that kind of support is paired with your own belief in yourself, there is no room in which you cannot hold your own.

As I grew in my career and stepped into leadership roles, I carried that lesson with me. It was not enough to find my own voice—I knew I had a responsibility to help others find theirs, too. I made it a priority to not just take a seat at the table, but to pull out chairs for others. I paid attention to who wasn't speaking up, who hadn't yet recognized their own brilliance, and I found ways to bring them into the conversation—just as someone once did for me.

There is something incredibly powerful about telling someone, "I want to hear what you think." It signals trust. It signals worth. It tells them they belong. Whether I was leading a team meeting or presenting to executives, I made it a point to spotlight the voices that needed to be heard. Not because they weren't capable of doing it themselves, but because sometimes the best kind of leadership is lending your credibility until someone finds the strength to stand in their own.

And as I did this, something beautiful happened—I built a circle of champions around me. A network of women and allies who had each other's backs, who passed the mic instead of holding onto it, and who believed deeply in collaboration over competition. That is what leadership looks like to me: showing up, speaking up, and making sure others are seen, heard, and supported. Because when one of us rises, we all do.

Leaders Don't Always Have the Title

Leadership does not always arrive with a title. Sometimes, it grows quietly—through your influence, your consistency, and the way others begin to rely on your voice. For a long time, I did not see myself as a leader in the traditional sense. I thought leadership had to be formal, assigned, or announced. But over time, it became clear that others were seeing something in me I had not yet fully owned. More than once, it was my coworkers—especially other women—who reminded me of the weight and reach of my voice.

One moment I will never forget was when a colleague I deeply respected pulled me aside while working on a major initiative. She had a vision, a clear plan, and the determination to see it through, but she also recognized that getting buy-in from the company's leadership would not be easy. She looked at me and said, "They listen to you. Your words carry weight here. I need you to speak on this with me." I was taken aback—not because I did not believe in the project, but because I had not realized just how much my voice had come to matter.

That gentle reminder changed the way I saw myself. Not just as someone who worked hard or showed up prepared, but as someone who could shape direction and drive decisions. Leadership, I realized, is not about being the loudest or most visible person in the room, it is about being intentional with your influence. It is about using your voice not just for yourself, but in the service of others. That moment became a turning point in how I carried myself and how I embraced the responsibility that came with being heard.

Find Your Superpower

As I stepped into my role as a leader, I understood that leadership is not one-size-fits-all. We all have a superpower—something that sets us apart, that draws people in, that fuels our ability to make an impact. For some, it is strategy or innovation. For others, it is empathy or calm under pressure. For me, it was my passion—and my ability to persuade. I could rally a room, energize a team, and inspire belief in a vision, even when the path was not fully clear. That fire, that unwavering conviction, became my signature strength. It was not something I learned in a textbook. It was something I had always carried—it just took time and reflection to name it.

Recognizing your superpower is transformative. It shifts how you show up. You stop comparing yourself to others and instead lean into what makes you powerful. When I stopped trying to lead like someone else and owned the strengths that came naturally to me, everything changed. I became more effective, more confident, and most importantly, more authentic. I encourage every woman—whether she sees herself as a leader yet or not—to dig deep and ask: What is my superpower? Because the moment you discover it is the moment you start leading on your own terms.

Owning your voice, recognizing your influence, and embracing your superpower is only the beginning. True leadership is a journey of continuous growth—and it starts with how you show up for yourself. I have learned that to lead others well, you must lead yourself first. That means investing in your development, protecting your energy, and setting boundaries that honor both your ambition and your well-being. Because while passion can fuel you, it can also burn you out if you are not intentional about how—and where—you spend it.

Investing in yourself as a leader does not just mean signing up for conferences, certifications, or reading the latest bestselling business book. Sometimes, the real investment is knowing when to step away, when to recharge, and when to model boundaries that empower both yourself and your team.

Work-Life Balance

Early in my career, I was fortunate to work for a boss who could see right through me. I was the first one in, the last one out, and never turned down a project. One evening, as I was buried in emails, he popped his head in and said something I will never forget: "Get out of here. Go home." It was not just a suggestion—it was a permission slip. He recognized what I had not yet admitted: I was burning the candle at both ends. His words reminded me that even the most driven leaders need people who help them protect their energy.

Leadership lessons do not always come from inside the office. One of the biggest wake-up calls came on a family vacation to Walt Disney World. While my kids were running off to meet characters and my spouse managed our perfectly planned day, I was glued to my laptop on a bench, answering emails. I was not really present, not for them—and, truthfully, not even for work. I told myself I was being responsible, but what I was really doing was avoiding the discomfort of disconnecting.

That moment sticks with me because it is the clearest example I have of what not to do. As leaders, we talk about balance, but living it takes intention. It is easy to over-identify with our titles or our inboxes. But our value is not in our availability—it is in our clarity, our decisions, our example. And you cannot set the tone for a healthy work culture if you are modeling burnout.

So how do you start setting those boundaries—especially when you have built your reputation on being available, responsive, and always "on"? Here is the truth: boundaries do not make you less committed. They make you more sustainable. More effective. And frankly, more respected.

Here are a few things that helped me shift:

Stop apologizing for being unavailable.

If you are off the clock, on vacation, or simply not responding after hours—own that. Leaders do not need to be "always available" to be taken seriously. Start by setting expectations with your team or clients: "I check emails between 8 and 6" or "I won't be available over the weekend but will follow up Monday." Clear beats constant.

Schedule yourself in. Literally.

Block time on your calendar for things that refill your tank—lunch, workouts, creative time, even family dinners. If it is not on the calendar, it gets bulldozed by the urgent stuff. Your time is a resource. Protect it like you would a team budget.

Do not just lead—model.

Your team watches what you do, not just what you say. If you are answering emails at midnight or skipping your own vacation, you are silently telling them to do the same. Set the tone by honoring your own limits. That gives them permission to do it too.

Redefine what "working hard" looks like.

Yes, hustle matters—but so does rest. Taking a break, logging off, or saying "not right now" is not laziness. It is leadership. It is prioritizing long-term performance over short-term heroics.

Ask yourself who you are trying to impress.

If you feel guilty setting boundaries, ask why. Often, we overextend ourselves trying to prove something—to a boss, a board, or even to ourselves. But the best leaders are not trying to impress. They are trying to influence—and that starts with showing others what it looks like to be whole, not just successful.

There comes a time in every leader's journey when the hardest, most courageous thing you can do—is walk away.

The Curve Ball You Didn't Expect

Up to this point I have been sharing the lessons I've learned about leadership: developing a strong work ethic, finding your voice, learning to lead others with empathy and clarity, building your own table, and making room for others at it. I have talked about how I evolved into the kind of leader I wished I had, discovered my superpower, and learned the importance of investing in myself—not just as a professional, but as a whole person.

But not every chapter of your life ends neatly. Sometimes, you can pour your heart into a role, show up early, stay late, give your best thoughts, and still be shown the door. I know, because it happened to m
e.

I left a stable, lucrative position to follow a leader I trusted—someone I had worked for in the past and believed in. It felt like the right move. I dove in, did what I always do: worked hard, gave my all, stayed committed. And then, out of the blue, I got a call that my services were no longer needed. No warning. No explanation. Just done. I learned later that the decision was not about me and more about the overall health of the company, however that was only after being pushed out the door.

It was one of the toughest professional moments I have ever had. Not because I had failed, but because I could not make sense of it. I kept asking myself: What did I miss? What did I do wrong? And then I realized—sometimes, it is not about you at all.

That experience taught me one of the most important lessons of leadership: you can do everything right and still not be someone's choice. And when that happens, you do not shrink—you stand. You pick yourself up, remind yourself who you are, and move forward. That moment did not define me—but it did become a defining moment. One that tested my resilience and ultimately reaffirmed my value. Over time I was thankful for the turn of events and realized God had a bigger and better plan for me.

As leaders, we need to know when to double down—but we also need to know when to walk away. Not out of bitterness, but out of clarity. When a place, a person, or a role no longer aligns with your values, your vision, or your worth, walking away is not quitting. It is leading yourself somewhere better.

Because leadership is not just about titles or teams—it is about how you choose to carry yourself through every season. The wins, the pivots, and even the painful goodbyes.

And now, I say to you: you are already leading—whether you know it or not. Lead bravely. Lead honestly. And when the time comes, lead yourself out the door with your head held high.

That, too, is leadership.

Christene Lankford-Grow

Christene Lankford-Grow is the founder of **Accelerated Growth Strategies**, where she serves as a strategic advisor helping consumer product brands expand into big-box retail, specialty distribution, and new market channels. With more than two decades of sales leadership experience, Christene is known for driving revenue growth, building strong customer relationships, and creating practical go-to-market strategies that deliver measurable results.

Throughout her career, Christene has worked alongside manufacturers, emerging brands, and established product companies to help them navigate the complexities of retail expansion. Her expertise includes retail readiness assessments, channel strategy, distributor placement, and sales team enablement. She works closely with leadership teams to evaluate whether their product, positioning, and infrastructure are truly prepared for large-scale retail opportunities.

Christene is also known for helping companies move beyond transactional selling by teaching teams how to engage in strategic conversations that lead to revenue. By focusing on solution-based selling, market positioning, and long-term partnership development, she helps brands strengthen their sales approach and accelerate growth.

As a trusted advisor, Christene partners with manufacturers and brand leaders to build scalable sales strategies, open new distribution channels, and position their products for sustainable success in competitive retail markets.

Connect with Christene

Website acceleratedgrowthstrategies.com

LinkedIn www.linkedin.com/in/chris-lankford-grow

What a Dog, a Coach, and a Dad Taught Me About Leadership

Angela Kesting

Leadership is more than a job title. It's how we move through a moment. In this chapter, I'll share a few everyday practices that have been helpful to me. Here are three short stories, three lenses: a dog who reads the room, a coach who knows the importance of showing up, and a dad who thinks in spreadsheets. Together, they reveal a simple throughline: awareness, presence, and connection.

Most of us have been on both sides of the coaching relationship—leading and being led, guiding and being guided. Leadership isn't about having all the answers. It's about being willing to stay curious, listen deeply, and keep learning. The best leaders and coaches I know invest in their own growth, because you can't help someone uncover their own insights if you aren't willing to seek them for yourself. My work has taught me that leadership is less about authority and more about awareness—about noticing your own reactions and responses while supporting others in doing the same.

My path to coaching hasn't been linear. I spent more than 25 years in corporate IT, building and leading teams and functions. I served as a board member and producer for a not-for-profit children's theater company. I taught yoga to collegiate athletes and volunteered in community settings. Each role taught me that what matters most is demonstrating your values in action.

Good leaders keep reflecting, expanding, and experimenting. They're not afraid to be challenged or to bring humor and imagination into their work—because creativity sparks new directions. Transformation doesn't have to feel heavy. It happens best when it feels like play.

Each of these stories touches on self-awareness, curiosity, presence, attuned coaching, and adaptability. Entire books have been written on each of these topics. My intention here is to introduce examples and illustrate how they can be woven together to strengthen the way you lead. Think of this chapter as an invitation to notice and experiment. Explore what resonates, try it out, and discover what works for you. Small shifts, practiced over time, can lead to meaningful change.

Awareness: My Dog is an Empath

Sometimes when I sit down at the computer, my dog Fitzy will get up from his bed near my desk and go lie down on the opposite side of the room. It's almost as if we were on a boat and he needed to balance out the weight on the vessel.

When I'm working on certain things and my energy subtly shifts toward frustration, intense concentration, or some other sort of activation that doesn't feel good to him, he creates space for himself.

He senses the tension in my body before I do. His movement away from me is often my first sign that I'm bracing. That my energy has changed: jaw clenched, shoulders creeping toward my ears, fingers hitting the keys with a bit more force. Oh, and if I say "agent" or "representative" on a phone call, he promptly exits, stage left.

Every time he does this, I'm reminded that energy matters, and *how* we carry *what* we carry matters.

Now, I cannot read this dog's mind. Maybe he's protecting his peace. Maybe he isn't. But I do know he's sensitive, like me. We both pick up on other people's energy. So, when Fitz shifts position, I take the cue. I pause, tune in, and resist the urge to rush. I ask myself what I'm feeling in my body and where—is it heavy or light, constricted or open, pinpoint or diffuse? Does anything feel stuck? Is there a sense of expansion or contraction, steadiness or shifting? My first step is to notice it. Then I can decide what happens next.

One of my favorite quotes—often attributed to Viktor Frankl, though its origins are debated—is: "Between stimulus and response there is a space. In that space is our power to choose our response. In our response lies our growth and our freedom."

Play with your newfound awareness and see if it's possible to shift anything—with breath, intention, perspective, movement. A little detached amusement helps. Employ a self-reflective sense of humor. Ask yourself: am I taking something overly seriously right now that perhaps isn't so overly serious?

I can think of many moments when I was rushing down a hallway, on my way from one meeting to another. And I wonder now what I must have been projecting energetically. What I carried with me from one experience to the next, infecting the new space with an old place. Was I flustered, rushed, distracted, annoyed, scattered, impatient? And most of all, was I centered only in my own experience? I cringe to think of how often this happened when I was supposed to be the leader in the room—of the team, of the meeting, of guiding us to a good outcome. Instead, I was unconsciously polluting the space. Now, I didn't walk into rooms screaming and shouting. I'm not even sure if my twisted-up energetic vibe was obvious to others. Doesn't matter. What's important is that I was unaware.

I'm not saying don't feel your feelings. Feelings want to be witnessed. They assert themselves for a reason and they'll keep finding a way to assert themselves until you pay attention. The important thing is to be self-perceptive and self-aware. If you are unaware, your ability to listen objectively or communicate well with others can easily get clouded.

Whether I'm quickly flagging something or taking time to thoroughly examine it, I follow this sequence: **Pause. Listen. Consider. Choose.**

First, pause.

That's your moment to check in with yourself, particularly to tune in to your body. I have found, much to my chagrin and after many failed attempts, that I cannot simply think my way out of a dysregulated moment. We may not always have the luxury of a long pause. But it doesn't have to be long. What matters is that it be conscious.

Next, listen.

Ask yourself: What am I noticing? What do I feel in my body? Where do I feel it? If it had words, what would it say? Weird, huh? Try it. You may be surprised at how quickly it speaks to you. And it's empowering to realize you may already have access to the answers and insights you seek. You just have to take a beat and clear space for them to emerge.

Then, consider.

What do I want to consciously carry forward into my next interaction? What do I want to release—at least until I have more time and space to process through it? What are my options here?

Finally, choose.

The choice could be as simple as recognizing your discomfort without rushing past that feeling. Then choose what you want to do. You could stop for a minute and press your hands against the wall. Or breathe in for four seconds, hold it for seven seconds, and breathe out for eight seconds. Perhaps you treat yourself to a dance break. Depending on the situation, your choice could take a variety of forms. Play. Be creative and curious. See what works for you.

Try this sequence in any situation and see what happens. Think of it as a science experiment. See if it changes anything about how you show up in work, relationships, parenting, decision-making, or even how you feel when you're waiting in line or stuck in traffic. You may find you get pretty good at going through the "Pause, Listen, Consider, Choose" sequence fairly quickly. At least quickly enough to be making conscious choices and not getting whipped around in the wind by things you didn't even realize were impacting you.

Don't have a lot of time to process whatever may be coming up? That's okay—as long as you note it and promise yourself that you'll revisit it when there is time and space to do so.

What I've described is simple—not always easy, but simple.

Now, other people may bring energy into a space that has you wanting to move to the other side of the room, à la Fitzy. We cannot control how others carry themselves in this world. What we can do is remember, with some measure of grace and compassion, that we all get caught up in our own web of messy energy sometimes. And the thing that often helps is employing a gentle curiosity, directed toward both ourselves and others. Ask yourself how you are doing. Ask someone else how they are doing. And be present for the answer.

One more thing for you on this topic—from a few decades back. When my son was three years old, he had a set of figurines from *It's the Great Pumpkin, Charlie Brown.* One of these characters was Pigpen, who was always depicted as moving around in a cloud of dirt. And the Pigpen figurine came complete with a dirt-covered ghost costume for Halloween.

One day after my son woke up from his nap, he was looking at his toys and said decisively, "Pigpen needs to clean his ghost, and clean himself." His tone and inflection were hilarious. It was even accompanied by two circular hand motions for emphasis. The only thing missing was the "Gurrrrl..." at the beginning of his sentence.

I remember thinking there was wisdom in this—how this statement could be a metaphor for making sure one isn't walking around leaving a trail of chaotic energy everywhere. Dust off your aura. Fix your frequency. Check your vibe. Mind your ghost, y'all. Clean your ghost. And if a thorough inspection and cleaning of your ghost isn't an option in that precise moment, I'd advise at least achieving self-awareness: know your ghost, know yourself.

Presence: Run on your Toes

In middle school, I ran distance for the track team. Very poorly, I might add. But I tried. My dad was a runner in his youth and competed in high hurdles. I was a short and slight kid, so hurdles were not in the cards for me at that age. But I could run on a flat surface without complete disaster.

Let's set the stage. It was 1983. My dad—with his worn white Hanes T-shirt, paint-stained faded jeans, black horn-rimmed eyeglasses (that I'm pretty sure were actually work-issued safety glasses he just wore all the time), and a wicked awful combover secured with way too much Aqua Net hairspray—was driving a rusted-out white Ford Pinto with orange trim and one red fender.

He was chain-smoking. At his feet was a haystack of chewed-up toothpicks and Stim-U-Dents in the driver's-side footwell—a sign of failed attempts to curb his cigarette habit.

This is how we'd train. I'd run. He'd pace me in the Pinto, coaching me. Periodically, he'd call out to me "Run on your toes!" as a cue to lighten my footfalls.

At first glance, this coaching setup may seem ridiculous. And it *was* ridiculous. It was also quite helpful, because I vividly remember it. He was completely present and focused on helping me: attuned, engaged, committed.

Would it have been better if he were out running beside me? I don't think so. From the car, he had a perspective that he couldn't have had if he was running. We could train for much longer this way. And I have to think this visual was even more entertaining for our neighbors.

What's the lesson here? Don't judge a book by its cover? Help comes in all forms? Smoking is bad for you? (P.S. It is.)

There are a few lessons in this—in how we show up for each other, in how we lead, coach, and connect.

First, **presence matters more than polish**. My dad didn't look the part. He wasn't the idealized version of a coach or even particularly healthy at that point in his life. But he showed up—in his own way, fully present, paying attention, staying with me. That's leadership. I felt important, valuable, and supported. How someone feels when working with you often sticks with them more than anything else. Stay present with the people you lead, help, and guide. Let them know they matter—and that helping them is the most important thing in that moment.

Second, **focus on what works, not what's ideal**. My dad couldn't run beside me, but he found a way to stay alongside me. Sometimes leadership means adapting the method to fit the circumstance, the moment, or the person. Don't get stuck on showing up perfectly. Just show up.

Third, **honor the effort, not just the outcome**. I wasn't a great runner, but he coached me anyway. I tried anyway. I finished every race anyway. Often last, but I finished. He taught me that trying matters. That time spent together supporting someone in their effort is valuable. And that seeing something through was important. There's power in honoring effort—your own or someone else's—especially when the win isn't guaranteed.

Fourth, **you never know the impact you may have on someone**. I'm not sure if either of us knew in the moment that we were making a memory. And that this memory would give me a sense of safety and settling in my nervous system. I was doing a thing that, by all accounts, could have provoked anxiety. I wasn't good at it. I was struggling to learn and improve, and it was hard. And still, I just remember feeling calm and supported.

Help people connect with what allows them to believe in their ability and potential. People may not always succeed at a particular task or role. But everyone has value and something to contribute. It's rare to find success right out of the gate. We will all try things and stumble. That's how we learn resilience and perseverance. You don't know how or where you'll succeed until you try different things. Having leaders, mentors, and coaches who are present through that process is invaluable.

Business outcomes matter. But the human-to-human impact we have is foundational. When we build trust and connection, positive outcomes tend to follow. Be tenacious. My dad knew I wasn't a good runner. It wasn't about the running. It was about me learning what a good coaching relationship looked like. It was about him supporting me through the process of building my confidence by committing to something, despite struggling or finishing in the bottom third. His investment of time and his belief in me gave me the courage to try other things—things I did succeed at—because I wasn't afraid of not being perfect. I wasn't afraid to try something that felt hard, uncertain, or uncharted. And to be supported and valued even when you are less than perfect—that's pretty great. Do that for someone. It matters.

Disclaimer: Please do not *literally* run on your toes. Your calves and your Achilles tendons will never forgive you.

Connection: Meet People Where They Are To Get Them Where They Want To Be

My dad's an engineer. He likes data, and he likes organizing it. I get it. There is comfort in bringing order to chaos. It can make you feel safe. Anything can have benefit if it's employed with awareness. For my dad, that means we employ spreadsheets. Liberally.

Ah, how my Virgo Sun soul sings at the opportunity to build a spreadsheet. And my dad uses them 100 times more than I do. He tracks all sorts of things: car service dates, budget numbers, solar energy usage, tax-related medical costs, his weight, his blood pressure, golf scores, a house-painting schedule, a breaker-box location key, home improvement projects. Once, he even made a spreadsheet to post above his spice rack with columns for the name of each spice, the bottle size in both ounces *and* grams, and comments. I promise you, the "comments" are the funniest part.

Even if it's not the best tool for the job, a spreadsheet is how his brain makes sense of information. That brings me to one of the biggest lessons I've learned in leadership and in life: the value of meeting people where they are.

A few years ago, my dad asked for my help on his journey to better health. At 82 years old, he's still actively working to improve his physical, emotional, and mental well-being. It's impressive. I have been humbled, and outperformed, on more than one occasion when accompanying him to an exercise class. Those senior citizens are not playing. And I love it. It gives me hope for myself, and for anyone who wants to stay active, strong, flexible, and balanced for all their years.

These days, I support him in many ways: as a second set of ears at medical appointments, as a coach, and as a partner in problem-solving. We are often more than 1,000 miles apart, but that does not slow us down. He likes to prepare for doctor visits by outlining key updates and questions, so we research, organize, and document that information together. We approach appointments with clear priorities and intentions, and walk away with actionable next steps. If something doesn't go smoothly, we typically know what to adjust. We work on self-advocacy with medical providers and constructively challenge anything that is unclear or inconsistent.

He wants to understand the "why" behind treatment decisions. So, I simplify and explain the mechanics and science behind medications, supplements, medical interventions, diet, nutrition, and exercise—often using metaphors that map to how he sees the world. I connect him with resources so he can do his own learning on specific topics. Once he has a clearer understanding, he can make informed choices about his health. And spreadsheets are the star of the show—something he can refer to when he needs a refresher.

If someone thinks in spreadsheets, give them a spreadsheet. Meet them where they are. I've found that people who seek coaching are already in a process of discovery, transformation, and self-challenge. They want to learn and unlearn certain habits and patterns. That's hard work. Find what helps them feel comfortable, clear, and safe as they approach that work, and meet them there.

People have different ways of understanding information and getting things done. Some prefer visual or auditory content. Some like to work alone on certain tasks. Others thrive in active collaboration. Some think best in stories or patterns. For most people, it's a mix of things. You don't have to pick just one. What works best can change depending on the task or the moment.

How do you—as a leader, coach, teacher, or mentor—accommodate this? Avoid assumptions. Ask questions and pay attention to what works and what does not. Be curious. Be open to different approaches.

Here are some things I consider and assess when working with someone:

What is the best format to use when sharing information with this person?

- **Audio-first**: Absorbing information best through conversation, podcasts, or voice notes.

- **Visual-first**: Preferring diagrams, charts, or color-coded notes over written text alone.

- **Text-based**: Needing to review written information to fully understand.

- **Kinesthetic**: Retaining information better by physically doing the task rather than watching or listening.

How does this person think?

- **Sequential thinkers**: Needing information in a clear, step-by-step order.

- **Big-picture thinkers**: Preferring broader context, the overall "why," and outcomes before the details.

- **Pattern and category thinkers**: Spotting trends, relationships, and themes quickly, often by grouping data into labeled buckets.

What works best for their memory and recall?

- **Story-based learners**: Understanding concepts better when framed in a narrative.

- **Analogy and metaphor processors**: Liking comparisons to familiar objects or scenarios.

- **Data-driven**: Wanting hard numbers, metrics, and evidence before making decisions.

- **Sensory anchors**: Remembering things by associating them with sounds, smells, or tactile cues.

What is their preference for interaction?

- **Collaborative processors**: Learning best by working together, bouncing ideas off others.

- **Independent processors**: Needing time alone to think before responding.
- **Rapid responders**: Processing ideas in real time during discussion.
- **Slow cookers**: Letting ideas simmer before they click, then responding with clarity.

As a coach, I might recommend an audiobook instead of a hard copy or provide a voice note or video recording instead of a white paper. We may work together on coaching exercises rather than having them complete things independently. I might construct a hands-on activity, schedule a walk-and-talk instead of a sit-down meeting, or incorporate music, art, or storytelling.

You may not be able to create a personalized experience every time. But when you have the flexibility, give it a try.

Ask people directly what works best for them. They may not know right off the bat, so create space for discovery. It's very empowering to know how you work best and to be able to ask for what you need. We are so often expected to fit ourselves inside systems: school classrooms, doctor's offices, corporate spaces, or organizational cultures that are not particularly curious, expansive, or flexible. As a result, many people haven't considered what may work best for them personally or even what the options could be. Give people an opportunity to discover and explore this as individuals and as teams.

Don't assume the person who has the loudest, quickest, or most polished answer always has the best one. If you are getting input from people in a group setting, consider using silent idea generation first with Post-it notes or digital whiteboard tools. Build in some pre-work prompts or pauses to allow more time for processing. Try round-robin techniques, small-group discussions, or breakout groups to create more options for contribution. You may be pleasantly surprised at the quality of ideas if you create conditions that make it easier for all perspectives to surface. You may see fewer miscommunications and have better buy-in and engagement across all team members. People who are actively involved typically feel more invested.

Most of us have standard ways of approaching things, and those are beneficial. Some of you may work in industries with strict compliance standards or other regulatory protocols. Those are there for a good reason. I'm not suggesting anyone throw templated approaches out the window. Have a structure. Have a toolbox of things you can pull from. But in the spaces where you do have flexibility, make sure you are not force-fitting an approach just because it's what is most comfortable for *you*. Ask questions, really listen to the answers, notice what you learn, and be adaptable and flexible. Be playful and open to new approaches. Try something and see how it works. Adjust if needed and try again. Failing isn't scary. Ceasing to learn and expand is scary. You don't only get the benefit of having a better chance at helping someone or achieving great outcomes. You get the benefit of climbing inside someone else's perspective and trying to see and experience the world through their eyes. This is an exercise that is critical for empathy, open-mindedness, and creating solid relationships.

Yep, my dad is attached to spreadsheets. But he isn't forcing anyone else to use them for their own stuff. He is clear on what works best for him. So, when he asks for my help, he asks me to share information in a spreadsheet when I can. That's him stating a need. And I can accommodate it. Most importantly, meeting people where they are helps them feel seen and understood. That builds trust and connection, a critical foundation for any work ahead.

The Throughline

These shared moments aren't prescriptions; they're reminders. Notice what's happening inside you, stay present with the person in front of you, and adjust your approach when needed to improve connection and communication.

Each story in this chapter offers a window into practices that can change the way you show up as a leader—in work, at home, and in everyday interactions. I've introduced them here so you can explore these tools, try them on, and see how they fit into your own life. These small shifts in awareness and behavior, woven together over time, can reshape the way you lead.

In these stories, my dad shows up both as the coach and as the one being coached—a reminder that leadership is fluid. We move between roles all the time, and each space we occupy has something to teach us. To lead is to learn, and to learn is to lead.

People don't experience leadership as stated hierarchy. They feel it in how you carry yourself, how you engage with them, and how well you assess and adapt to the circumstances. Leading from within really does start with the "within"—so clean that ghost, show up, and tune in. That's how awareness turns into growth, and growth turns into impact.

Angela Kesting

Angela Kesting is the founder of **AJK Coaching, LLC,** where she helps people and organizations navigate change with clarity, steadiness, and practical insight. With more than twenty-five years of experience in global corporate technology—including leadership roles in strategy, operations, product, digital marketing, and organizational transformation—she brings a blend of technical depth, systems thinking, and human-centered guidance to her work.

Angela provides life, health, and professional coaching as well as business consulting—all customized to meet the unique needs of individuals and organizations. Her approach integrates reflection, curiosity, empathy, creative problem-solving, and manageable next steps—supporting clients working through career transitions, health challenges, life disruptions, or simply the sense that something is out of alignment.

Angela holds multiple certifications, including Reiki Master, Mental Health First Aid, Six Sigma Green Belt, and Luma Institute Certified

Practitioner of Human-Centered Design. She's taught yoga to collegiate athletes, with a focus on injury recovery and prevention. She's a former board member and producer of a Chicago-based not-for-profit children's theater company. She currently volunteers with the Reiki Brigade, supporting its mission to promote peace and serve groups experiencing high levels of stress, including first responders, veterans, front-line workers, and communities in need.

Connect with Angela

Website ajkcoaching.com

LinkedIn https://www.linkedin.com/in/angelakesting/

The Calling That Wouldn't Let Go: How Loss Sparked Leadership

Michelle Valiukenas

Dealing With the Unimaginable

"If you want to make God laugh, tell Him your plans."

I never realized how much that quote would apply to the direction my calling and my journey took, both personally and professionally.

Let me introduce myself. I am a mom of three—two angel babies and one living child. I have worked in nonprofits my entire career, as a practicing lawyer and now as a founder and executive director of The Colette Louise Tisdahl Foundation (CLTF). A few years into my career, I realized that my passion was nonprofits, not law, so I got my master's in nonprofit management at DePaul University, where I met my husband,

Mark. We both joked that we would never start our own nonprofit and preferred working with existing organizations. In 2018, for various reasons including the focus on growing our family, I found myself at a career crossroads, uncertain of my next move.

After infertility, IVF, and miscarriage of "Sweet Pea" at 8 weeks, I was finally in my second trimester of pregnancy. I submitted my resignation at 20 weeks pregnant, giving about 12 weeks' notice to help find and train my replacement. I planned to be a stay-at-home mom for this long-awaited baby. That joy was short-lived. At 21 weeks, something told me to see my OB. Little did I know that this decision would completely alter my life's trajectory.

During the routine vitals, my blood pressure was 188/110. After Mark and I heard the heartbeat, we were sent to the hospital's labor and delivery department. A nurse took me into a room, ushered me into a gown, and put a fetal monitor on my belly. Things moved quickly. There was difficulty with finding Colette's heartbeat on the fetal monitor and then with finding her on the ultrasound. I was told to relax because my blood pressure was too high, and then finally that I was being admitted, with no explanation, none of which were helping my blood pressure.

Later, when Mark went home to let out our dog and I was alone, the on-call OB finally explained I had severe preeclampsia and would be admitted until delivery. It was May 8th, and my due date was September 7th. I texted Mark the news who responded, "you're kidding." My response: "I'm not creative enough to come up with this."

The next day, I notified work, family, and friends. Two doctors visited—a kind, empathetic neonatologist and Dr. McScary, an appropriate nickname for the maternal fetal medicine doctor who struck fear during our 20-week ultrasound. They launched into numbers and statistics; our emotions made it nearly impossible to process the information. The one thing we did understand: 24 weeks, what they called viability, was when they would intervene medically. If she was born before then, we would get to hold her, and she would die in our arms. We became obsessed with viability, marking off the days on a giant wall-calendar in my hospital roo m.

After that first day, I got into a routine of work, blood pressure checks, doctor visits, TV, and taking short walks. After a day or two, I realized I was privileged enough to handle this upheaval financially and that those who could not say the same needed help. I told my husband, who sighed and said, "Please, for once, could you think of yourself and our baby and not everyone else?" My response: "You know who you married."

After three weeks, a repeat ultrasound led to an emergency C-section and at 24 weeks and 5 days, Colette Louise Tisdahl entered the world.

Before the delivery, everyone warned us that her size meant we would not hear her make any noises. Once Colette was out, the room got quiet. Then, I heard this tiny, but powerful squeak. I asked, "Is that her?" and they responded "Yes!" in surprise.

I heard Colette saying, "Mom, I've got this."

Colette went straight to the NICU and then Mark went to see her. Eventually, complications with my surgery required I be put under because of the more intense needs of the surgery, despite the risks. I survived, but scars remained.

Colette's nine days in the NICU were a rollercoaster of ups and downs. Mark would either stop at the NICU or call the nurses on his way to work. He would report back, and I would head to the hospital, then we would have some time together as a family before heading home for the night.

On the morning of May 31, 2018, Mark called me, but it was different. I could hear Mark's voice trembling. He sighed and said the doctor told him they had to resuscitate Colette last night.

At the hospital, the doctor saw me and said "Oh, good, mom is here. Yeah, let's go find a space to talk."

I thought, *I don't want to do this, I'm not ready. Please let me wake up from this nightmare.*

In the room, I was too paralyzed to sit. The doctor said they had done everything. As he talked about the risks of her size, I screamed, "*Why was I so focused on viability, on 24 weeks, when it didn't matter?*"

Unable to breathe, I kept telling myself that this doctor had no idea how powerful my daughter was. In my state of pure denial, I imagined that years from now, with Colette still alive, we surely would laugh at this story.

The doctor finally finished, but before he did, he said "Do you believe in baptism?"

I mumbled "Yes" and he said, "Well, it's time."

I realized he expected Colette to die. That is what baptism meant.

Shaking and crying, I called Mark, telling him to come.

I went to her room thinking, *Colette, you've got this, prove them all wrong.*

The hours ticked by as our family gathered. With two minutes until shift change, when hospital rules barred any visitors, a nurse said, "Mom, you better come with me." Mark was already in Colette's room. I walked with her, noticing it was eerily quiet; as I passed staff, they gave me forced and awkward smiles.

The nurse opened the Isolette. Mark and I touched and talked to Colette through tears until Colette was baptized and the doctor took all her wires off.

We entered the room with our waiting family. Everyone made way for us to hold Colette. I took her into my arms first. I held my gorgeous baby for the first time and finally without wires and tubes. We held and talked to her, then so did the rest of our family. Everyone cried. Then we held her again.

After a while, the doctor checked her heartbeat. My breath caught, would she pull through? The doctor finally stepped back, lowered the stethoscope and said, "She's gone."

Let's Do Something About It

The days after Colette died were a blur. My sister planned her memorial. All I wanted to do was sleep, to escape the reality of my daughter's death.

Despite the grief, the thought of a financial assistance program for families navigating a similar path kept gnawing at me. I wanted and needed to do something in Colette's memory, with new mom energy and no baby who needs it. Giving back is in my blood so this seemed perfect. But, I was grieving, awash in self-blame and questioning. Although I had a vision, I wanted someone else to do it despite the clear need I saw. In my grief, I felt like I failed and blamed myself, saying that I had killed Colette. The grief, imposter syndrome, and fear of failing made me feel like I was not capable.

To convince myself this was not my path, I went to talk to hospital social workers; they all were eager to help me with this new endeavor. Friends and family reaffirmed I could do this. I wanted to do something, to help others, to keep Colette's name and memory alive.

Finally, despite self-doubt, fear, and grief, I realized this was my calling and how I would parent Colette. It felt as if Colette's squeak was now saying, "Mom, you've got this."

On September 7, 2018, Colette's due date, I took the leap and launched The Colette Louise Tisdahl Foundation, a nonprofit that would provide financial assistance to families dealing with high-risk and complicated pregnancies, NICU stays, and loss.

I naively thought that I would go to a hospital, introduce my organization, and be welcomed with open arms. The hospitals' red tape made it a struggle to get to the right person. Luckily, Janet, the head social worker of my delivery hospital, believed in us. She became a vital supporter because she shaped our applications to the best possible and her team were our first referral sources.

Our journey was complicated and required creativity. I quickly realized we had to do more than financial assistance. First, there was a lack of education and awareness. Simply sharing my story, and what helped and what did not, made an impact. A year into the organization, a former boss saw me at an event and said that a family friend had had a loss and to figure out how to best help, she and her daughter-in-law went back through the organization's social media posts. We educate on topics relating to poverty, to NICU, to parenting after loss, to grief and loss, and so much more.

I also started to notice the systemic problems. Our applicants shared how they did not qualify for any sort of leave so taking time off work to see their baby in the NICU was not feasible or that pregnant people would neglect medical advice in order to work. I saw the true impact of not having federal paid leave. So, we now partner with other organizations to work towards change.

The start of the organization was slow. We had to get frontline staff to trust us. Our first request for financial assistance finally came in mid-November. A family with a child in the NICU at the same hospital that Colette was at applied seeking help. Helping that family and then hearing their relief was a boost personally as well as to our mission.

We would help a family here and there, but no matter what I did, we could not seem to gain momentum. I cried a lot during the first year-plus. It felt wonderful to help families, but then no one would apply, and I would feel the same overwhelming guilt and shame that I felt over Colette's death—as if I were losing her again. I remember saying to my mom, "I just need this to work."

My time and focus became getting the word out. I talked to anyone willing to listen; I commented on Facebook posts for NICU and loss families sharing a financial need, I found others serving a similar demographic and shared our work. Slowly, but surely, people were hearing about us and trusting us.

Suddenly, about a year and half in, the application floodgates began to open. Families nationwide applied, seeking help for all their expenses—transportation costs, car payments, rent, phone bills, utilities, funeral expenses, and more. We now average about 50 to 60 applications for help per week and the need far outweighs what we can do these days.

Today, seven-plus years later, we've helped over 3,500 families across the country, at least one family in every state, with more than $1.9 million in assistance to families navigating the three stages of Colette's life: high-risk or complicated pregnancy, time spent in the neonatal intensive care unit (NICU), and loss of a pregnancy or baby.

Right now, my main priorities are raising awareness of our work so that we can get connected to donors and supporters, which in turn allows us to help more families. To do this, I network regularly, maintain and develop new relationships, write articles, appear on podcasts, lead presentations and training, and share my story and the stories of the families we have helped.

I love that I get to say Colette's name constantly and parent her differently than I imagined but still filled with love. But the work can also be triggering, infuriating, and sad. No matter how many families we help or what kind of impact we make, grieving for Colette will never end.

I tend to focus on how much more work is left, but I also recognize our accomplishments and the difference we make. In an optional follow-up survey sent three months after receiving help, more than 80% of our families say that the impact made a significant or total difference in their lives. That is Colette living on.

Superheroes Are Closer Than You Think

Once the initial dust settled after Colette's death, my husband and I talked about our next steps. We still very much wanted a child, but we were scared and grieving. Ultimately, I realized I was terrified to be pregnant again and wanted to use a gestational carrier.

Just like he always has, Mark jumped onboard. In May 2019, we started on a surrogacy journey that resulted in my only living child, Elliott, born in July 2020.

The surrogacy journey was beautiful; not only did our family grow with Elliott, but with our surrogate and her family as well. Elliott loves including our surrogate in the story of his birth, almost as much as he loves talking about his big sister Colette.

A few days after we found out our surrogate was pregnant, I broke down crying, saying we had made a mistake. I desperately wanted this baby, but I also grieved the loss of carrying this pregnancy and feared not being able to bond with my baby.

With the help of my therapist, other parents who had used a surrogate, and my research, I created rituals to make me feel connected despite not being the pregnant one.

The second I held Elliott and looked into his eyes I was instantly bonded. I spent most of the first night staring at him, marveling that this is our baby who I get to hold and take home.

I am honored to be Colette's and Elliott's mom. I always introduce myself as a mom of three, two angel babies and Elliott, who has the energy of all three. I am honored to do the work I have done (and will continue to do). I do not regret listening to my call and starting this organization.

Elliott and Colette are the loves of my life and my absolute best teachers. Plus, the love they have for each other is so heartwarming and beautiful.

My relationship with Colette goes beyond the foundation. She speaks to me in so many ways. Most of my ideas of how to give back come from her. She also knows how to pull the best pranks, from hiding my necklace which mysteriously showed up in a place I had checked multiple times once I started crying, to the little patch of mud right by my car door at the cemetery, to the mail addressed to the foundation that gets returned, even though the address and the postage are correct.

Elliott reminds me to be curious, to have fun and be silly, but also be incredibly caring and loving. His answer to "what do you want to be when you grow up?" is Superhero, and he believes it is his job to protect people. He even called me a superhero for my work with the foundation, a compliment that stays in my heart. He is now our Director of Hugs, a job he treasures, which was created for him after he very sweetly asked me, "Mom, what's *my* job with the foundation?"

Elliott may call me a superhero, but the truth is that anyone can step into their own Superhero role if they are willing to listen and act. The question is how we do that.

I have no magic answers, no epiphany, no aha! moment. The process involves three distinct steps: (1) listening to that message; (2) identifying the issue or problem; and (3) doing something about it.

First, I was confronted with a heavy truth, that pregnancy can go awry. While I was able to afford a long hospital stay, I knew so many others would have to make tough decisions based on finances. I heard and continued to hear the message that I needed to do something about it.

Second, I knew there was a problem. Some families could not prioritize their family's health simply because there was not enough money. These crises could happen to any family and when the average American lives a $400 crisis away from total financial ruin, this would continue to be an issue.

Third, I figured out what I wanted to do. I did my research first and then looked at whether I had the resources and bandwidth to do this. Then, I took the scary leap and said, *I have to do this*.

Let's say you are reading this and thinking, *I want to start a new organization or initiative.* Great, kudos, and I would love to hear all about it. But ask yourself some questions: Can I work on this initiative full-time? Do I know what I need to know? How much time do I have to dedicate?

I am incredibly grateful and privileged to have a supportive partner and the financial means to make this a full-time job, without drawing a salary. If the calling is loud enough, you need to figure out what you can do with what you have. Psst, it does not have be a brand-new endeavor. Let us look at some examples of problems and various levels of bandwidth.

Scenario #1: You are dropping your kids off at school on the coldest day of the year. You notice many kids are not wearing weather-appropriate coats. You keep having the image of kids shivering outside and realize you are being called to do something. You decide to host a coat drive where parents can donate old coats and accessories for families to shop for free.

Scenario #2: In your neighborhood, there is a dangerous intersection. One day, after you almost have an accident there, you hear the call that you need to do something about it. You circulate petitions for stop signs to be placed at that intersection, then take those petitions to the next town hall and request stop signs.

Scenario #3: You are educated about your community's rampant food insecurity. The closest food bank is almost an hour away via public transportation and has limited hours, rendering it inaccessible to those who need it most. You set up and run a community food pantry, getting volunteers and donations to help those in need.

All of these scenarios came from the simplest first step: listening and being receptive to hearing it, identifying a problem, and coming up with a workable solution. We can all listen to our callings and then do something.

Despite many telling me that I am doing something heroic or amazing, at the end of the day, I am a mom whose experience opened her eyes to other families and the gaps in services and who then did something about it.

So, are you ready to open yourself up to these messages? Are you ready to follow your calling into action? Best of luck, and I hope to hear all about your accomplishments.

Michelle Valiukenas

Michelle Valiukenas is the founder and executive director of **The Colette Louise Tisdahl Foundation (CLTF)**, a national nonprofit dedicated to supporting families facing high-risk and complicated pregnancies, NICU stays, and loss. A longtime nonprofit advocate and self-proclaimed "recovering attorney," Michelle's life—and purpose—shifted forever after the loss of her daughter Colette, born at 24 weeks and held for the first time at nine days old, only moments before she died. In her deepest grief, Michelle felt an unshakable calling to act. On Colette's due date, she launched CLTF to ease the financial burden for families in crisis and to honor her daughter's brief but powerful life.

Under Michelle's leadership, CLTF has grown from a single idea scribbled in a hospital room to a national lifeline that has provided more than $2 million in direct financial assistance to over 3,800 families across all 50 states. Today, Michelle is a sought-after speaker, writer, and advocate who partners with healthcare systems, social workers, mental health providers, policymakers, and community leaders to advance awareness, education, and systemic change in maternal-infant health.

Michelle is also a proud mom of three—two angel babies (Sweet Pea and Colette) and her living son, Elliott, who serves as CLTF's "Director of Hugs." She credits both Elliott and Colette as her greatest teachers, guiding her work, her parenting, and her belief that every family deserves support, dignity, and compassion during life's most vulnerable moments.

Connect with Michelle

Website colettelouise.com

LinkedIn www.linkedin.com/in/michellevaliukenastisdahl

Leadership Knows No Age

Becca Berkenstadt

The first time I knew I was a leader was when I was in seventh grade, and I felt I had suffered a huge injustice in my young, impressionable life.

It was spring of 2000, when a teacher, one that did not impress my 12-year-old brain, tripped over a backpack and fell. I am sure she was embarrassed and sore, maybe even hurt. (I have compassion for her physical injury, not her ego.) Her response to this incident was not to ask the student whose backpack she tripped over to make sure to keep his backpack under his seat or on the back of his chair but to leave the classroom, march down to the principal's office, and ask for a ban on backpacks.

I wasn't quite sure exactly what happened next, but I know the principal had some sort of discussion with other teachers and they agreed that when walking through the paths between the desks they too had tripped and were fed up with students' backpacks being in their way.

What came next was an extreme response to a minor annoyance—an annoyance that had very easy fixes from my perspective. They wanted to ban backpacks, and they told us that it would happen in a few short weeks. Fireworks went off in my mind. When I heard I wouldn't be allowed to bring my backpack to class, my mind screamed WHERE AM I GOING TO STORE MY TAMPONS SO THAT THE BOYS WOULDN'T SEE THEM?! I was in the throes of puberty and as you can imagine it was awkward, embarrassing, and at times straight-up surprising.

I felt betrayed. I felt combative. And I was going to do something about it.

That night over family dinner, I asked my parents—one of them a lawyer—what I could legally do to "fight the power." I learned about petitions, peaceful protesting, negotiation, and the impact of public relations.

After dinner, on my Windows 98 PC, I set out to create a Word document with a grid layout. This petition template was the first piece of the puzzle. I asked my dad to print out a few copies of my design and borrowed a clipboard for school the next day.

Over the next 48 hours, I got over 100 signatures! It turned out there were many students that didn't want to give up their backpacks. I am sure there were a myriad of reasons students signed my document and not *all of them* were worried about the dreaded tampon exposure, but I know that was a concern of at least a few other girls. I was standing up for the underdog and the rights of my fellow students.

The next week I staged a sit-in in our library. I passed secret notes throughout all my morning classes with the details of that afternoon's sit-in. I made sure not to sign my name, but I am pretty sure the principle knew it was me who had created this ruckus. When fifth period rolled around, about 25 students met in the library and sat in a circle created using tables and bean bags. We just chatted and waited. Nothing happened. We thought we had won! First a teacher walked by and gave a confused glance and then a few minutes later the principal came. He asked what we were doing. I proudly stood up and said, "We are having a peaceful protest. We don't want our backpacks taken away." He laughed. That infuriated me. I explained that we were serious. He sternly told us to go back to class. A few kids started to get up. I told them to stay seated. The principal and I were in a standoff. I asked him if he would listen to us and allow the students to keep their backpacks and get rid of the deadline. He then bellowed, "Get back to class!" All the students scattered, and I sulked back to class.

That night at family dinner I told my parents what had happened. After the meal, my dad and I got on the phone with his friend Jay, a cameraman at the local news station. Later that week, Jay was at my school filming a group of my friends (the backs of our heads) wearing backpacks as we were walking out of the school after the dismissal bell rang. It was glorious! The news reported on my sit-in and the ongoing struggle between the students and the administration on what could only be deemed as "Backpack-gate."

Unfortunately, we still weren't where we needed to be. The principal had kept the deadline for the backpack ban in place. I took one last shot. Once again, I sat down at my Windows 98 computer and typed. I wrote a professional letter to the principal stating facts and citing instances that highlighted our need for backpacks including my signed petition, peaceful sit-in, and the negative publicity that this issue was causing the school. My ask... a town hall meeting where concerned students could attend and share their thoughts, feelings, and proposed solutions to the administration.

The next morning, I hand-delivered the letter to the admin gatekeeper for the principal. I waited patiently while the principal deliberated on his decision to host a town hall.

I couldn't believe it; my request was (I am sure, begrudgingly) granted! The town hall meeting took place a few days later, one hour before classes in the gym. It was all the time we needed to plead our case. We walked away hopeful and heard. Two days later the impending doom of the backpack ban deadline was lifted. We had won!

That experience made me into the leader I am today. I followed a process, I kept fighting even when it looked like defeat had struck, I was consistent, and used my credibility as a straight-A student to persuade the necessary parties of my rights and my ideals, and all while I was authentically me.

How do I embody this 12-year-old girl as a business owner today? Let me tell you.

As I am writing this chapter, I am 17 years into owning my digital marketing agency, Worldly Strategies. You can bet that I have learned a thing or two after marketing over 40 different businesses in a wide range of industries across the world.

Credibility is a major factor when it comes to marketing a business and securing clients. It's the first thing that I evaluate when I start working with a new client. Credibility is highly based on consistency and authenticity.

I find that if my client is having trouble with consistency, it's because they either don't know who their customers are or they haven't defined the values for their company. Sometimes they even adopt a completely different marketing persona that doesn't reflect their authentic self. Having a separate persona for your work or business that's different from who you really are can lead to frustration, anxiety, annoyance, fear, embarrassment, and burnout. That's how many business owners or marketing directors feel when they come to Worldly Strategies for help with their marketing growth plan. In the back of their minds, they are saying, "Where is my company headed? How can I connect with my audience?"

These questions can be daunting. It's like asking, "Who am I? How do I get people to like me?"

I help clients define their dream customers by analyzing their three favorite past clients and extracting the characteristics that made those relationships feel aligned, rewarding, and successful. They can even be creative and add a few characteristics they *wish* these past clients emulated. This exercise aligns the business owner's or company's values with the type of customers they want to work with. When you know your audience's likes, dislikes, fears, and reveres, then you can connect with them on a different level, a level where they feel seen. If they feel seen, they will trust you and buy from you.

Clarity starts with you. When you understand your values, your ideal client becomes obvious. Self-awareness sharpens audience awareness. This is how you sell to the *right* people.

Now that you have been given a taste of the methodologies I use to help a business owner or company find clarity, let's dive further into my three-step process to becoming an authentic leader.

Step 1: Get to Know Yourself

What defines you? What are your values? How do you want to impact the world?

Sometimes answering these questions simply takes time. Sometimes, hiring a therapist for yourself or a marketing agency for your business can get you where you need to be faster than if you tried to do it all on your own.

I am not ashamed to say that over the past 17 years I have been in business I have asked for help many times both personally and professionally. At different times I have hired a business coach, therapist, time-management coach, and more. There is strength in asking for guidance. With each subject matter expert I hired, I learned more about who I was and what I wanted for my life.

I distinctly remember a cold, wintery day in 2018 sitting in my therapist's office on an orange retro-style couch with a pile of blue laminated words. My therapist asked me to look at each word and carefully evaluate if the word defined me as an individual. After I had split the stack into two distinct piles—my values and random words, I narrowed down my values to 10 specific words. Together we talked through why I thought these values were a part of who I was. This exercise was invaluable because I walked away understanding what I was looking for in relationships with friends, family, business partners, and clients.

Once you understand how you want to show up in the world and in your career or business, it is easier to answer those three questions above.

Below is a list of ways you can get to know yourself better:

- Travel by yourself.
- Journal about your life experiences, your hopes, and your feelings.
- Look at a list of values and circle 10 that align with you most.
- Hire a coach or a therapist to guide you through exercises or discussions that will build self-awareness.

A note on traveling by yourself. During my last two years of college at DePaul University in Chicago, Illinois, I saved as much money as I could from my internship so that I could accomplish my goal of living and working in another country. As soon as I graduated (I didn't even walk at graduation), I got on the next flight to Sydney, Australia, booked myself into a hostel within walking distance from most of the iconic, landmark sites in the city, and started looking for a job in my field of digital marketing. I went halfway around the world, away from everyone and everything I knew to start the process of truly becoming an adult.

After about a month, I found a position at a company called Blackglass. I became their Paid Search Account Manager. This job then funded my next two and half years of self-discovery. I ended up traveling by myself to every major capital city in all five Australian states and two Australian territories. This gave me an unbelievable perspective on my life and the world. I was no longer a student living and working on a campus somewhere in the United States. I was a tiny ant amongst a bustling colony, trying to find my place.

Traveling alone allowed me the freedom to try new foods, clothing, and activities without judgment from external sources. It also allowed me to experience new cultures and how they chose to connect with the world around them. Lastly, I was essentially proving to myself I was strong enough, smart enough, interesting enough, ENOUGH. I wanted to know myself, value myself, and accept myself. I craved independence, renewal, authentic connections and experiences, confidence, clarity, and personal growth. Many of these cravings are my core values today.

I recognize that I have a major privilege to be able to concoct this outlandish plan of traveling and working abroad but if you have the time and money to travel alone, even for a weekend to a new place, I highly recommend it for self-discovery purposes.

If you don't have the time or the funds to travel, try journaling for 10 minutes each day. Write about what you are grateful for, your goals, and your wins for the day. Don't just stop there though. Dive deeper. Describe experiences that brought you joy and ones that brought you pain. What did you feel in those moments? Fleshing out these experiences and your feelings will allow you to learn more about yourself and what you value. You will also learn what situations and obligations no longer serve y ou.

Another great exercise you can find online and print out is a values activity. Google "list of values." Next, select 10 words that align with your personality and your future goals. Then take these values to a coach or a therapist and talk through why they are important to you.

Sometimes it isn't enough to process everything on your own; talking to someone who specializes in problem-solving and analysis can be beneficial.

Step 2: Build Credibility

Credibility is derived from consistency and authenticity. People are drawn to leaders that don't apologize for who they are.

I love to laugh, make jokes, be silly, and love my life but I also can slow down, listen, contemplate, sit in the uncomfortable, and be serious. I don't need to "turn on" or "turn off" my personality and neither do you.

In business and in life, you will find the people who are right for you. You will naturally gravitate to friends, colleagues, clients, and power partners who share your same values. That is why it is so important to know who you are, what you care about, and what you want out of the world, then embody those traits consistently.

Below is a list of examples that can help you build credibility.

- Answer texts and emails within 24 hours
- Arrive on time
- Set clear expectations
- Set clear boundaries
- Do what you say you are going to do

- Post on LinkedIn at least once a month (business owners and professionals)
- Join professional groups or non-profit boards

Let's break down how each one of these actions can build credibility. Answering texts and emails promptly and arriving on time proves to people that you are reliable. Setting clear expectations allows others to plan accordingly and show up at their best. Setting clear boundaries demonstrates that you respect yourself. When you do what you say you are going to do, those around you feel safe because you are predictable.

Posting on LinkedIn once per month tells LinkedIn that you are a person on their platform to elevate. This is a way to market yourself and comply with the LinkedIn algorithm. People want to know if they check LinkedIn, you are real, a thought leader, active in a social setting they assign value to. In 2026, it is *THE* platform for professional connections. Don't skip posting on it at *least* once per month if you want to get ahead in the world of business.

Joining a professional group or nonprofit board increases your exposure to experienced professionals, opening the door to new opportunities for learning and career growth.

Ok, let's discuss what happens if you are busy and can't answer a text or email within 24 hours because let's be real, this happens. Apologize, take accountability, and make the situation right. It is as simple as that. All these behaviors build trust. With many jobs going overseas or to younger graduates that cost less to employ, if you want to stand out in business, make sure you can check the boxes above.

Step 3: Execute Your Chosen Goals

I am a firm believer in setting and accomplishing goals to move my life and my business forward with intention.

I do also give myself permission to change my goals as I grow. Life is long and as I evolve, I find my core values may shift slightly, my desires change, and, therefore, my goals must adapt as well. What I cared about as a 12-year-old was certainly born out of a fiery passion for privacy over my bodily functions, but today I am an open book when it comes to my reproductive health. This is because I am no longer embarrassed by natural biological functions and instead value helping other people by sharing personal stories and experiences.

I have always believed in fighting for my rights, protecting my freedom, especially as a woman, and helping people. As a 12-year-old, that advocacy was rooted in self-protection and privacy. Today, those same values show up differently: I still fight for autonomy and freedom, but now I do so with the intention of helping others by sharing my experiences and creating space for honest conversation.

Below are some ways you can be more successful setting and executing your goals.

- Once a year, write down your goals.
- Hang them up where you can see them on a regular basis.
- Break down your goals into bite sized, achievable tasks and

timeframes.

- Consider hiring someone to help you achieve your chosen goals faster.
- Each time you achieve one of your goals, reward yourself.
- When creating a new habit, aim to practice it for at least six weeks. If you miss a day or a session, get back to it as soon as possible. Realize that new habits take time to establish.
- If your goals are habit-based, try habit stacking. Link a new desired behavior to an established one. For example, if you want to floss every day, start doing it right after brushing your teeth.
- Try using a journal with goal prompts. I use "The Five Minute Journal." You can buy it on Amazon.
- If your values shift or desires change, adapt your goals to match.

Over the last 17 years my values have shifted, and I have aligned my goals to match. In 2021 I wanted to have a child. This idea was foreign and scary to me. I didn't know how being a mother would affect my business that had long been my only child. I asked questions such as, "Will I still have time to serve the same number of clients? Will my business continue to grow? How will I handle the responsibility of having a child and running a business?"

Through business coaching with Kim Kleeman of Accelerate Successfully, I learned that with the right strategies in place, I could continue to run and grow my business. I hired additional staff. I networked closer to home or on Zoom so that I could spend less time commuting and become more efficient with my connection efforts. I became a leader of a local professional moms' group which allowed me to meet more business owners and potential clients in an organic way. I prioritized time with my son and now being a mom is a great connector for me in my business communities. My values shifted from working on my own and traveling for fun to working as a team, staying closer to home, and spending quality time with my family.

Leadership knows no age. There is a saying that you are either born a leader or become a leader. I believe that you can be born a leader, but the trait doesn't emerge from your being until there is a catalyst, until there is a need that inspires your mind, body, and soul to act.

I am a fourth-generation business owner. Entrepreneurship and leadership have always been a part of my personality and my identity at its core. I was taught as a young leader how to impact change and how to do it the RIGHT way. This was demonstrated in the story I shared above.

As a 12-year-old, when you stand up for a cause you believe in, it is usually met with strife from adults. I am sure I was viewed as a defiant, annoying pipsqueak that doesn't know anything about the world. Well, I am still that 12-year-old today. I am methodical, challenging, a trailblazer, strong, funny, smart, organized, and an authentic LEADER. If you have the confidence to be the best parts of your 12-year-old self, you will be able to be your authentic self as an adult. When you are in boardroom, at an investor pitch meeting, on stage speaking about your expertise, let yourself know you have that 12-year-old warrior inside of you.

If you have children, nieces, nephews, kids you mentor, friends who are young biologically or young mentally, let them know that leadership can be found and honed at any age. It is a power inside of you and there is three step process to setting this power free. Every day that you walk on this earth, you are given the opportunity to grow, change, and accomplish your goals. Take advantage of this short time you have been given and live the life you want.

Something my father always said was, "You only get one body and one life." Now, most of the time he was talking about safety issues like rough housing, but I knew that he also meant life is what we make of it. It can take you 30 years to get to where you want to be, but when you arrive, the feeling will be oh-so-sweet.

If you have dreamed of writing a book, starting a business, getting your health on track, speaking in front of a crowd, etc. now is the time to start working toward that dream. There is no better day to start than today.

Becca Berkenstadt

Becca Berkenstadt is the founder of **Worldly Strategies**, a North Shore-based digital marketing agency that has been fueling growth for businesses for over 17 years. Worldly Strategies is an experienced results-driven, globally-minded digital marketing agency. We implement online marketing strategies. Our core services include Social Media Management, Online Advertising, Search Engine Optimization (SEO), Email Marketing, and Website Design. A Google Certified AdWords Professional, she also holds certifications from DePaul University and Sydney University in various marketing disciplines.

Beyond her professional accomplishments, Becca is a dedicated community leader. She founded and manages the rapidly growing **Highland Park/Highwood Professional Moms** group, which has gained over 600 members in just one year. As a former President of the Professional Women's Club of Chicago, she continues to support and empower women in business. Becca is also a professional speaker, delivering actionable marketing strategies to business owners and leaders.

Her career journey has taken her across the globe. Becca has lived and worked in Madrid, Spain; Sydney, Australia; and various U.S. cities, gaining diverse marketing experience. Her background includes roles at leading marketing firms such as Networked Insights (now audience.ai), Blackglass in Australia, and Kennedy Communications in Madison, WI, providing her with a global perspective on traditional and digital marketing.

Giving back is a core value for Becca. She donates 5% of Worldly Strategies' annual profits to the Domestic Abuse Intervention Services (DAIS) in Madison, WI. Additionally, she serves as Secretary of the Cremer Foundation, which funds grants to nonprofits supporting at-risk communities, including the homeless, hungry, and victims of abuse.

Becca lives in Highland Park, IL, with her husband Kyle, their son Henry, and their dog Jelly Bean. Originally from Madison, WI, she brings Midwestern values of hard work and community spirit to everything she does. Her extensive marketing background and passion for supporting communities make her a trusted partner for businesses seeking bold, results-driven strategies.

Connect with Becca

Website www.worldlystrategies.com

LinkedIn www.linkedin.com/in/beccaberkenstadt

Building a Community: Your Ultimate Business Strategy

Natalia Duarte

What I Want for You

Investing your time and energy in building a community is one of the most impactful ways to create the life you want. My hope is that by the time you finish this chapter, you feel both convinced and empowered to become a community builder. This is not only because it is good for your well-being and because it is what our society desperately needs (and a beautiful way to be of service), but also because it will position you as a leader and give you a platform to accelerate your business in ways you could not achieve on your own. Through this often overlooked marketing strategy, you will find a way to build trust with your customers and, ultimately, loyalty, which is the most valuable thing you can earn from them. Furthermore, by finding thoughtful monetization strategies, your community can become self-sustaining or even turn into an additional source of income.

Hear me out… One of the painful lessons the COVID-19 pandemic taught us is that we do not function well in isolation. Social media, once celebrated as the great connector, has actually helped fuel a loneliness epidemic. We are a deeply social species, and to survive and thrive, we need community.

In *The Good Life: Lessons from the World's Longest Scientific Study of Happiness*, Robert Waldinger and Marc Schulz share the results of a decades-long Harvard-led study. Deep, meaningful relationships are the most powerful determinants of happiness, health, and even longevity. The problem is that we are getting worse at being around people. We hide in the comfort of our devices and our headphones, even though studies show that you come out of something as simple as a train ride feeling better if you interact with others than if you spend the ride fully isolated.[1]

People are in desperate need of opportunities to have positive, real-life interactions. There was a time when religion helped meet this need for community, but fewer people are gathering in places of worship. For a while, shopping malls became the place to see and be seen, but brick-and-mortar retail is quickly becoming a thing of the past. So where are people supposed to gather now and fill this need for connection?

That is where we come in. Leaders who know how to bring people together and help them create strong bonds are essential in our modern world, where people are actively looking for new ways to connect and find a sense of belonging. I have seen this need up close.

My life has been full of change and of intentional efforts to build community wherever I go. I was born and raised in Mexico City, then moved to Atlanta, Georgia, to pursue an MBA. I got married and moved to Toronto, Canada, to support my husband's career. After that, we lived in Minnesota, Arkansas, Pennsylvania, and now Illinois. It has been a journey.

Every move has brought its own challenges and has helped me develop my networking skills. Three years ago, we moved to Evanston, Illinois, with our three kids and have finally settled. I knew I had to hit the ground running. I immediately started reaching out to people, organizing dinners at home every weekend, and approaching every interaction with curiosity. It did not take long to feel like we had a good group of friends to rely on.

When it came to developing a professional network, things were harder. I did not know where to start and attended a few networking events without much success. I was lucky to meet Tami Palmer through a mutual friend. She has built an amazing community of working moms in the Park Ridge area, northwest of Chicago. It is such an engaged and supportive group that, alongside Kim Kleeman, they have expanded the concept throughout the Chicagoland area and beyond, creating the Professional Moms Community Network (PMCN). Tami and Kim trusted me with building the Evanston Professional Moms chapter, and it has been such a fun endeavor. I have met supportive, interesting, and brave women who inspire me every day and make me feel like I belong. I wish the same for you.

In the following pages, I will share examples and reflections on how to build a strong community by changing your mindset to become an effective leader, how to use this platform for your business, and how to monetize it to create extra income.

A Change of Mindset: from Salesperson to Leader

I see you. I have talked to you and I understand you. Yes, you. You do not consider yourself a leader and you have tried your best to sell, but it feels uncomfortable. You have thought to yourself, "I hate selling." You are an introvert and feel drained every time you leave a networking event. You have followed the marketing gurus and joined the game of creating content for YouTube, Instagram, and Snapchat, but it is simply not you and it is exhausting. You know what you love to do and the kind of life you want, and you wish you could just do that without having to put yourself out there so much.

Changing your mindset from being a salesperson to being the leader of a community can give you the boost you need to increase your sales without constant awkward self-promotion. Let me tell you about Tony.

Tony has been a music teacher at an elementary school for fifteen years. He is also a father of two young children. He loves working with students, but lately he has noticed himself feeling less patient and more drained. Around the same time, a change in leadership at his school increased uncertainty for several teachers. All of this got Tony thinking about starting a new stream of income on the side.

At first, he was unsure what to do. Then he remembered a conversation about music with a friend's father, who was blown away by Tony's knowledge of music history. This friend suggested that Tony should teach music appreciation classes for adults, especially older adults with time on their hands who would love to learn more about music.

Inspired, Tony put together a program exploring styles from Stravinsky to The Doors. A few people registered and really enjoyed the sessions. After the program ended, he received enthusiastic feedback and was asked to develop new material.

That is where he got stuck. Tony struggled to stay in touch, keep people engaged, and attract new attendees. He hates reaching out to people to offer his courses because he feels uncomfortable acting as his own salesperson. He also dislikes posting ads on social media and knows nothing about creating marketing campaigns.

Tony and I talked about his struggles, and I recommended that he start a public Facebook group. Even though he was reluctant, he decided to try. He named his group Melómanos Le Club and invited friends, family, and former students to join. He began posting links to things he found interesting, like a Leroy Anderson piece for typewriter, along with engaging questions, such as asking members to share the song they listened to over and over again when they were teenagers.

Soon, people were interacting and sharing their favorite music. It did not take long before some members started coordinating to go to concerts together. Tony stepped fully into the role of the leader of this group. The visibility helped him increase attendance at his music appreciation programs, and he even started teaching private piano lessons to some group members, creating extra income for his family. Even more important, this community gave him a way to connect with other music lovers, make friends, impact the lives of others, and create a real sense of belonging.

This mindset shift from salesperson to leader was a true game changer. It did take time and commitment. At first, Tony had to post frequently and sometimes felt like he was screaming into a void. But once the momentum started to build, it was worth it. He began to see tangible results in the connections he was building and in the lives he was touching. After being a shy seller for so long, this impact gave Tony the confidence to offer his courses. It became easier because he had already built credibility with his audience. His group saw him as the expert, as the leader.

A Community is a Network with a Soul

Networking is a great way to get new leads and clients, but it can often feel transactional. How many times have you gone to an event and collected a stack of business cards without forming a single real connection? You might be great at networking, getting referrals, and amassing LinkedIn connections, yet still never feel part of a community. In a nutshell, a network is about connections, while a community is about relationships. A network has common goals. A community has shared interests and values, and most importantly, a sense of belonging.

When I lived in Pittsburgh, Pennsylvania, one of the moms at my kids' elementary school started a Buy Nothing Facebook group in our neighborhood. Buy Nothing groups are local spaces where members post things they no longer need and give them away to whoever replies. The idea is wonderful because it keeps things out of landfills. In most groups, though, the same people claim things repeatedly and others never get a chance to participate.

I have belonged to a few of these groups, and it usually goes the same way. That is, until I joined one in the Squirrel Hill neighborhood, where the administrator's vision of community building changed the dynamic of the whole group.

Cosy, the admin, started with a clear goal of building a conscious and kind community, not just a transactional network. Her strategy was to educate us. She posted the rules consistently and welcomed new members. When people joined, Cosy reminded us of the importance of something she called "simmering," which meant waiting a few days after posting to give everyone a chance to reply, then choosing the person who would receive the item. You could choose randomly or by any creative method, such as asking people to reply to a particular question and then selecting your favorite answer. With Cosy's system, we got to know each other and built trust.

There is one interaction that captures the feeling of this community. A neighbor shyly posted a long piece of elastic. She had bought it for a project and never used it. She doubted anyone would want it but decided to offer it anyway. She wrote that she would choose who to give it to, based on how each of us would use it.

I replied that I could use it to play with my girls. There was a game I used to play in Mexico with my friends during recess. Two players stood apart as "posts" with the elastic band around their ankles. A third person jumped in and did a little choreography. If she did it flawlessly and jumped out without mistakes, the "posts" moved the elastic up to their knees, and then the final challenge was around their waists. It was a fun, healthy, and entertaining game that I wanted to teach my daughters.

The person who posted the elastic loved my response and chose me. Then another neighbor replied to my comment asking about the game, because she had played something similar as a child in Poland. That simple post made me feel closer to two of my neighbors.

Through these interactions, I got to know my neighbors better, not only by exchanging items, but by hearing their stories and finding surprising things in common. The group became so engaged that we started getting together in person and organizing neighborhood garage sales. It grew so much that Cosy eventually had to split it into smaller areas and assign new administrators.

She had no problem finding people willing to help, but many of us were disappointed not to have her as our admin anymore because she had become more than that. She was now the respected leader of the group. That, to me, is a true success story of community building.

Now, you might be thinking this is all great, but how does it connect to your business? Let's get to that next.

Your Ultimate Marketing Strategy

Community building might sound like a *pro bono* project, but I have seen it work as a brilliant marketing strategy. Beyond all the benefits it creates for society and for your own well-being, it is important to highlight three valuable business opportunities.

Community creates a space to learn about your target market. Take Blanca, who has loved dogs her whole life, especially her four-legged "son," Patch. She launched a business selling dog-themed merchandise but struggled to stand out because the competition was fierce. Her first strategy was to start an Instagram account and post like crazy. After several months of posting, she had only reached a handful of followers. She was disheartened, because she is an artistic person and she knew her posts were good. She had gone through something similar with a coffee business before, and she did not know what to do next.

We talked about switching her strategy to community building, and everything shifted. There are so many dog lovers looking for people who share this passion. Through Blanca's community, people shared their proud dog photos, asked for advice from other owners, and recommended grooming salons and vets. But most importantly, these online conversations gave Blanca invaluable feedback about what her target market cared about most and helped her redesign her online store. Creating this community proved as an invaluable platform to learn about her target market and adjust her product design to meet their needs.

Community gives visibility to you and your business. The most obvious way to monetize your community is through the people who are drawn to your business because of it. For example, my mentor, Tami Palmer, is a career coach and the leader of the Park Ridge Professional Moms group, mentioned at the beginning of this chapter, which has been around for more than ten years and now includes more than five thousand women. I am always impressed to see how every time someone posts a question about handling a promotion request or preparing for an interview, members immediately refer them to Tami. She does not even have to promote herself. Others do it for her, because she has positioned herself as the leader and career expert in the group and is top of mind.

Similar things happened with Tony, who sold out his music appreciation courses through his group, and with Blanca, who now has a successful platform to sell her dog products, because they are recognized as experts and leaders in their area.

Community creates opportunities for additional sources of income. Being a leader in a community takes time and effort. Some might think that the leader should not be paid, that this work should be done purely as a service to society. I see it differently. I believe that making sure the leader or organizer receives at least some kind of remuneration is the best way to ensure the community can be sustainable and stay alive in the long term.

Once your group is big enough, there are several monetization strategies you can apply. A big one is having a "sponsor of the month," where companies interested in your target market pay a monthly amount in exchange for a mention, a shout-out, or a post within your group. It is also important to start gathering your members' email addresses from the beginning. This way, you can design a newsletter to keep them informed about upcoming events and news from the group, and you can offer a newsletter sponsorship as well.

If you organize meetups or events for your group, that is another opportunity to generate income, either from event sponsors or by charging a ticket fee. A paid member directory might be another idea. As you can see, there are several ways to monetize your community, either to cover your organizing costs or to generate an additional profit.

What Has Worked for Building Evanston Professional Moms

As I mentioned in the beginning, I am the founder of Evanston Professional Moms. This group has become a way to bring together everything I have learned about building community throughout my life. In just eight months, it has grown to 400 members. We host consistent monthly meetups that usually bring together 16 to 20 women. We send a monthly newsletter with highlights from our events and a Member Spotlight section that features one woman from our group each month. This month we are also launching our sponsorship program for 2026.

Here are a few strategies that have worked especially well in building the Evanston Professional Moms community:

Get people engaged. Our main channel of communication is Facebook. Even though it is not a perfect platform, it has worked well to bring people together and keep the conversation going. What works best for us is posting polls and simple, interesting questions so people have an easy way to respond and interact. Over time, you start to notice what your group enjoys and what sparks conversation. At the beginning, you might need a few friends to jump in and answer your prompts, but it is wonderful to see when members begin responding to each other and making their own connections.

What I like about this strategy is that it creates buzz and organic growth without burning you out trying to feed the content machine. You do not have to become an "influencer" who posts at the speed of the algorithm. When you are building a community as a marketing strategy, you can still create content, but the priority is helping members feel comfortable participating, sharing, and commenting. Your role is to be present, to set the tone, and to gently keep things moving instead of carrying all the weight yourself.

Even the language we use is telling: "followers" versus "members." In one case, people passively consume your posts in a mostly one-way broadcast. In the other, there is a two-way street where relationships can grow. This distinction matters even more now that the game is changing. For years, the question was, "How much attention can I get?" Now, trust is the real currency. Anything you do to increase trust increases your customers' loyalty and your value. You can buy attention through ads and paid influencers, but that does not guarantee loyal clients. People want more than a transaction. They want to feel seen, to belong, to be part of something bigger. Community building is a powerful way to do that, and focusing on engagement is your most effective tool.

When you start your group, you might think the most important measure is the size, but you quickly realize that what really matters is engagement. I have seen small but active groups become solid and highly effective communities. Focus on helping members feel comfortable posting questions, recommendations, comments, and shout-outs, and on encouraging them to interact with each other. That kind of participation will naturally grow your numbers, bring people to your events, give you the platform you want for your business, and eventually attract sponsors' interest.

Get people together. In my Evanston Professional Moms journey, there was a pivotal moment when we started organizing in-person monthly meetups. Online groups can have a great impact, but deep and meaningful relationships really start to grow when you meet face to face. Once people have spent time together in real life, their online interactions also become kinder and more supportive. Even if your group is spread across different places, try to organize local meetups with whoever is nearby.

Do not worry if only a couple of people show up at first. Keep going. Plan ahead and post events a month or two in advance so people can add them to their calendars. The key is consistency. Keep organizing and inviting. Little by little, the community will respond. And remember to post photos from your events so others realize they want to be there next time.

We first started meeting at cafés, and that worked well in the beginning. However, as the group gets larger, it can be noisy, and you might end up "stuck" just talking to whoever is sitting next to you. What has worked well for us is asking members who have space to host our meetups. Using this strategy, we have gathered at a photo studio, a realtor's office, the city hall offices, just to name a few. Hosts provide snacks and drinks, which gives them visibility within the group and makes everyone feel pampered.

Get people to share. One of my favorite tools for this is our Member of the Month spotlight. Each month, I choose a member who has been active in the group, someone who has been posting, commenting, or showing up regularly. I send them a few simple questions and ask for a photo. Their answers and picture are then featured in our Facebook group and in the monthly newsletter.

This spotlight creates engagement, because people know that when they participate, they are more likely to be featured. But getting members to share their story also builds a real sense of community. Instead of only seeing ads or promotional posts, members feel like they are getting to meet friends, not just contacts.

Another strategy that has worked beautifully is what I call the magic question. When I first started going to networking events, I noticed how transactional many of them felt. You walked around collecting business cards and hearing elevator pitches, but it was hard to remember who was who. Names and job titles fade quickly, but stories stay with you. Since my main goal was to build community first and trust that business would follow, I decided to change the dynamic.

At our meetups, we form a circle and go around with introductions. Each person shares their name and what they do, but they also answer a magic question. This is a question that people are excited to answer and just as excited to hear others respond to. It does make the introductions a bit longer, so I remind everyone to keep it short and simple. The payoff is worth it. People discover unexpected things in common, the room relaxes, and strangers start to feel like friends. By the end of the meetup, there is usually a lot of laughing, swapping stories, and genuine connection.

Finding ways to help people share, whether through a member spotlight or a thoughtful magic question, has been one of the most effective ways to turn a loose group of contacts into a real community.

See You on the Other Side

Building a community is one of the most powerful ways to share your message and grow your business. It is also one of the best ways to live a healthier, more connected, and more fulfilling life. Research and experience show that strong communities bring lasting benefits for your health, well-being, and long-term happiness.

For me, community building has been a great platform to understand the business landscape in the Chicagoland area. It has given me the chance to listen to working moms, receive honest feedback, and clarify which business to launch. Thanks to this experience, I have identified key pain points for working moms and am preparing to launch in 2026 a subscription business of ready-to-eat family dinners delivered to your door within Chicago's North Shore.

Throughout this chapter, you have met different people who might not have seen themselves as leaders at first, but who took a leap of faith to build a community around something they cared about. The impact on themselves, on those around them, and on their businesses has been real and visible. Patience and consistency are key. Think of your community as a small plant. Tend to it regularly. Give it care and attention, and watch it grow, evolve, and become something beautiful and self-sustaining. The journey is worth it, and the rewards are extraordinary.

The world needs fewer influencers and more community builders. I hope you will join us. See you on the other side.

NOTES

[1] This idea is supported by two strands of research: the *Harvard Study of Adult Development*, led for many years by Robert Waldinger, which shows that close relationships are the strongest predictor of happiness and health over a lifetime, and experiments by psychologists Nicholas Epley and Juliana Schroeder, who found that commuters who talked to strangers on trains reported feeling better than those who stayed in silence with their devices.

Natalia Duarte

Natalia Duarte is a bilingual MBA graduate with a background in business, talent development, and instructional design. Earlier in her career, she worked in leadership development and helped design programs, coach professionals, and build strong organizational cultures. But life took her across countries, cities, and communities, and through those moves she discovered a deeper calling: creating connection to build stronger communities wherever she goes.

Now settled in Evanston, Illinois, Natalia has become a dedicated community builder and is the founder of **Evanston Professional Moms** (part of the larger **Professional Moms Community Network**), a local network that creates meaningful spaces for women to connect, support one another, and grow in both life and work.

She is also the founder of **Time2Savor**, a ready to eat family dinner service launching in May 2026 for busy working moms. Through healthy, comforting meals, Natalia hopes to help families reclaim dinnertime as a moment of peace, presence, and connection.

Connect with Natalia

Website: time2savor.com

LinkedIn: www.linkedin.com/in/nataliatopeteduarte

When I Lost My Voice, I Found My Leadership

Simona Pappalardo

There are moments in life when everything you thought defined you suddenly disappears.

Not gradually. Not politely. But all at once.

The title that introduced you in meetings. The role that structured your days. The certainty of knowing how to answer the simple question: "So, what do you do?"

When those things fall away, something unexpected happens. You are left facing a much deeper question:

Who are you when the labels disappear?

I did not expect to confront that question on International Women's Day. And I certainly did not expect to confront it without a voice.

Entering the room felt harder than it should have been. Eighty women were gathered for an International Women's Day luncheon, filling the wine bar with conversation and laughter. Plates clinked, chairs scraped, waiters squeezed between tightly packed tables.

And I stood there, unable to say a single word.

The irony was almost absurd. I had spent two decades building a career around leadership—speaking, presenting, inspiring teams across continents. Yet on that day, the day meant to celebrate women's voices, I had none.

Just a few days earlier I had lost something else too—my job.

After twelve years of building what many would have called a dream career, I had received the call: the company was restructuring, and there was no longer space for me in the executive ranks.

To be honest, the news did not come as a surprise. I had sensed the writing on the wall for months. When my boss's boss finally called, part of me even felt relief.

Over the previous decade, the organization had given me extraordinary opportunities, and I will always be grateful for them. But during the final year, the momentum had changed. Market pressures, economic conditions, shifting consumer behavior—many forces beyond anyone's control—were shaping decisions. No single person was at fault. I hold no resentment.

Still, when someone calls to tell you that you no longer have a job—especially when you have had one continuously since graduating from college—the moment lands with a force that is hard to describe.

I had always been considered top talent. I had been rewarded financially and professionally. I had built a reputation as a leader.

And suddenly, none of that seemed to matter.

There was an additional layer of irony that was difficult to ignore. My final day at the company would fall on International Women's Day.

Earlier in my career, one of the most meaningful recognitions I had received was being selected—along with only nine other employees out of a global workforce of seventy thousand—to fly on the company's private jet to New York for a gala hosted by a prominent organization advancing gender equality. The trip was meant to recognize my work supporting women's advancement within the organization.

Apparently, such achievements are easily forgotten when the cold mechanics of corporate restructuring take over.

Losing Voice, Gaining Perspective

Yet the real challenge I faced was not the job loss itself. It was something much more immediate.

I had already purchased my ticket to the luncheon months earlier. There was no way I would skip it. But attending meant networking—and networking meant answering the inevitable question:

"Simona, what do you do?"

Without my impressive title, who was I?

And just when I thought the situation could not become more ironic, it did.

The morning before the event, I woke up with a sore throat—and completely voiceless. Not hoarse. Silent. I could not produce a sound.

Losing my job title had shaken my confidence. Losing my voice shook me to my core. Should I even go? What was the point of celebrating alongside other women if I did not know who I was anymore—and could not even speak to them?

For a moment, staying home with a mimosa felt like the most reasonable alternative.

But I went. I showed up. Feverish, slightly disoriented, and unable to speak, I walked into the room.

As I approached the venue, I had hoped I might at least whisper. But once inside, the noise level made that impossible. Communication through voice was simply not an option.

I scanned the room looking for a familiar face, but the movement of people made it difficult to focus on anyone for more than a few seconds. Women stood in small clusters, leaning toward each other over glasses of champagne, laughing, exchanging business cards, introducing friends and colleagues.

Fragments of conversation floated through the air: A startup that had just secured funding. A consulting business expanding internationally. A nonprofit initiative gaining momentum.

Normally I would have stepped confidently into those circles. Networking has never intimidated me. After twenty years presenting strategies to executives, facilitating global meetings, and leading complex discussions, introducing myself at a luncheon should have been effortless.

Yet that day, it felt completely different. Without my voice—and without the professional title that had accompanied me for more than a decade—I suddenly felt as if the familiar script guiding those interactions had disappeared.

Who was I supposed to be in that room now?

For the first time in many years, instead of stepping forward to introduce myself, I stepped back, listened, and observed.

And so, something unexpected happened.

Slowly, being voiceless began to feel like a gift. I observed the women around me: business owners, founders, leaders who had built their careers on their own terms. They were confident, self-sufficient, and unapologetically ambitious.

Only days earlier, I might have looked at them with admiration from a distance, but thinking they were on a very different path than mine. But by sitting there in silence, another possibility emerged: What if my career did not need to continue along the course I had always known?

What if, instead of returning to lead engineering organizations inside large corporations, I allowed myself to imagine something totally different?

What if I listened to the quiet nudge telling me to become my own person? What if leadership did not require a title?

What if leadership could be expressed in life itself—the kind that people follow not because they must, but because of what someone represents?

And suddenly I remembered something I had written a decade earlier during my very first management training: my leadership legacy statement. It read:

"To provide energy and inspiration to everyone, myself included, to dare more, to step out of one's comfort zone and to reach new personal heights."

That statement had guided my decisions for years. And in that moment, I realized something profound. It did not tell me how I had to live my life. But it described exactly what living at my best looked like. My compass. My true north.

Title Leadership vs. Identity Leadership

What I eventually discovered is that there are two very different kinds of leadership: Title Leadership and Identity Leadership.

Title Leadership is the one most of us think of first. It comes with an organizational chart, a team, a budget, and a job description. Your authority is recognized because your role says it should be.

Identity Leadership works very differently. It comes from who you are at your core, what you stand for, and the consistency between your values and your actions. People follow Identity Leaders not because they must, but because they want to.

Titles can disappear overnight. Organizations restructure. Careers pivot. But identity remains.

That realization was both terrifying and liberating. If leadership lived in my title, then I had just lost it. But if leadership lived in my identity, then nothing had actually been taken away from me.

I simply had to choose to step into it again.

Start With the End in Mind: The Nobel Story

One of the stories that has always fascinated me is how the Nobel Prize came to exist. Some historians debate whether the details are exactly as the legend tells it, but the lesson behind the story remains powerful.

In 1888, Alfred Nobel—chemist, engineer, and inventor of dynamite—experienced something most of us will never encounter: he read his own obituary while he was still alive.

His brother Ludvig had died, but a newspaper mistakenly believed Alfred himself had passed away and published the obituary under his name.

The headline reportedly read: "The Merchant of Death Is Dead."

The article criticized Nobel for having made his fortune through explosives and weapons. It painted a portrait of a man whose legacy would be tied to destruction rather than contribution.

Imagine that moment for a second: you are reading how the world intends to remember you—while you still have time left to change the story.

For Nobel, that moment became a turning point. Deeply disturbed by the idea that his life's work would be remembered in such a way, he rethought the impact he wanted to leave behind. When he eventually wrote his will, he dedicated the vast majority of his fortune to establishing prizes that would recognize people who advanced humanity in fields such as science, literature, and peace.

Those prizes would later become known worldwide as the Nobel Prize.

I often think about that moment because most of us will never read our obituary while we are still alive.

Yet the question it raises is one we should all ask ourselves long before the final chapter of our lives is written.

Leadership Without Title

During my twenty years in corporate life, I heard the phrase constantly: "Everyone is a leader." I repeated it many times to my teams. But if I am honest, I am not sure I truly understood what it meant. Ironically, it took losing my title to discover the answer.

After leaving my corporate role, I began interviewing for other senior positions. On paper, many of the opportunities were impressive. They were influential roles, well compensated, and filled with challenges I knew how to navigate.

And yet something felt *off*.

Each conversation followed a familiar pattern. The leaders interviewing me were intelligent, thoughtful people. They clearly saw the value of my experience—the scale of the organizations I had led, the global complexity I had navigated, the teams I had developed. From the outside, the fit seemed obvious. But every time I closed my laptop after an interview, a quiet discomfort remained. It was not that the roles were uninteresting, earlier in my career I would have accepted them without hesitation.

But something inside me had shifted.

The questions they asked me were about the same types of problems I had already solved, the same structures I had already navigated, the same organizational dynamics I knew intimately.

Instead of feeling energized, I felt as if I were being invited to replay a chapter of my life that had already reached its natural conclusion. Slowly, I began to realize that the discomfort was not coming from uncertainty about my abilities.

It was coming from clarity about something else: the next chapter of my life was not waiting inside another corporate office.

Then I began my work as a leadership coach.

Day after day, I met with people standing on the edge of their own metaphorical cliffs. Some lacked clarity about what they truly wanted. Others knew exactly what they wanted but lacked the courage to pursue it.

Watching these moments unfold led to a realization that changed my understanding of leadership completely:

Titles may grant authority, but only identity creates leadership.

Leadership is not a position. Leadership is the willingness to act.

It is the ability to find, deep within yourself, the energy required to take a step toward the future you desire—even when uncertainty is present.

It is the moment when you decide to bet on yourself. Not because success is guaranteed, but because doing nothing would mean abandoning the life you want to live.

Not everything you attempt will work. But refusing to try guarantees that nothing will change.

Own Who You Are

There are eight billion people on this planet. And there is only one you.

You can seek advice from parents, friends, mentors, or colleagues—and sometimes their perspectives are incredibly valuable. But the reality is that what works for them will not work for you in exactly the same way. Your experiences, your values, your context, and your aspirations are uniquely yours. And the pace of change in the world today only reinforces this truth. Strategies that worked last year may not work this year.

At one point in my corporate career, I had roughly 150 people reporting into my organization, spread across four management layers beneath me. Only my direct reports interacted with me frequently enough to observe how I thought, how I made decisions, and how I approached problems. Everyone else experienced my leadership indirectly. They were also located across multiple countries and continents.

So how do you lead people you rarely see? How do you inspire individuals who may never sit in a room with you?

The answer is simple, but not always easy.

You lead through who you are. Through your values. Through what you stand for. Through the culture you create.

Culture moves through organizations in ways that are often invisible. As the anthropologist Edward T. Hall famously wrote:

"Culture hides more than it reveals, and strangely enough what it hides, it hides most effectively from its own participants."

I have felt this truth personally.

Over the course of my career, I have lived on three different continents, and I am married to someone from a culture very different from my own. These experiences have placed me in situations where something seemed obvious to the group around me—but strikingly unusual from my perspective. What others saw as "normal" was simply the culture they had always known.

And this insight fuels much of the work I do today. On one side, I coach expatriates navigating the complexity of living and working across cultures. By helping them understand cultural dynamics, communicate effectively across borders, and build confidence in unfamiliar environments, I enable them to accelerate their careers, secure promotions, and create opportunities that translate into tangible financial and professional rewards.

On the other side, I work directly with leaders and teams—whether in small startups or mid-sized businesses—to uncover the invisible elements shaping their organizational culture. Through practical workshops and coaching sessions, we strengthen collaboration, improve engagement, and align behaviors with business goals, helping companies unlock higher productivity, innovation, and ultimately, stronger financial performance.

Culture is the DNA of a team. And if you want a team to perform at its highest level, you must first understand the cultural forces influencing how people think, communicate, and make decisions.

Two Years Later: Still Becoming

As I write these words, another International Women's Day is approaching.

Nearly two years have passed since that crowded luncheon where I sat silently in a room full of accomplished women, unsure of who I was without my job title.

In those two years, I have spent far more time answering a different question.

Not "What do you do?" but "*Who are you?*"

The answers have led me to write a book—*Authentically Yours*, to build a coaching practice, and to share my work with leaders across cultures and industries.

Looking back now, there is a poetic irony in the way that transition began. The moment that forced me to rethink my entire identity started with losing my voice—literally.

At the time, it felt like terrible timing. How could I attend a networking luncheon when I could barely produce a sound? How could I introduce myself to anyone when I wasn't even sure who I was anymore?

And yet, that silence became one of the greatest gifts of that day.

Because when you cannot speak, you listen differently. You observe more carefully. You notice possibilities that might otherwise be drowned out by the noise of your own explanations, defenses, and rehearsed answers.

That day, surrounded by eighty women celebrating their achievements and their ambitions, I realized something important: **voice is not only about speaking. Voice is about alignment.**

It is about the courage to live in a way that reflects what matters most to you, even when the path ahead is uncertain.

Finding your voice does not happen in a single moment. It is a lifelong process of discovering, losing, and rediscovering parts of yourself.

And perhaps that is the real privilege of leadership—not the authority to direct others, but **the responsibility to continually become more fully yourself.**

And yet, becoming yourself is rarely a straight path. If anything, life seems to specialize in placing us in moments that challenge the very identity we thought we had carefully built. A job disappears. A project fails. A plan that looked perfectly mapped out suddenly dissolves. The roles we relied on to define ourselves—executive, expert, manager, founder—shift or vanish, sometimes faster than we can process.

When that happens, it can feel as if the ground beneath us has moved. But perhaps those moments are not interruptions to our path. Perhaps they are the path.

Because **when the external labels fall away, something much more important has the chance to emerge: the question of who we are when nothing is holding the mirror for us.**

That question is not comfortable. In fact, it can be deeply unsettling. For a while after losing my role, I caught myself instinctively reaching for my old title in conversations, as if it were a passport that allowed me to enter certain rooms.

Without it, I felt strangely exposed.

But slowly I began to realize something that in hindsight seems obvious: the people who were drawn to work with me were not responding to a title. They were responding to something else entirely.

They were responding to energy. To conviction. To the willingness to ask difficult questions and to walk alongside them as they searched for answers.

None of those things required a job description. In fact, in many ways they required the opposite: the freedom to show up as a human being first, and as a professional second.

This realization changed the way I began to see leadership altogether.

Leadership, I came to understand, is not something that lives in organizational charts or reporting lines. It lives in the invisible space between people—in the trust we build, the courage we model, and the possibilities we help others see.

A title can amplify influence, but it does not create it.

And when the title disappears, what remains is the truest measure of the leader you have become.

Two years after that voiceless International Women's Day luncheon, my life looks very different from what I once imagined. I am no longer leading large engineering organizations. I am no longer navigating the internal dynamics of global corporations or managing hundreds of people across multiple continents.

Instead, I spend my days working with leaders who are standing at their own crossroads—people who sense that something in their professional life no longer fits, but who have not yet found the courage to redefine what comes next.

Every time I sit with a client who is wrestling with that uncertainty, I think back to that crowded wine bar, to the headache, the fever, and the strange blessing of not being able to speak.

Because **sometimes the moment that feels like the loss of your voice is actually the beginning of finding it.**

And perhaps that is what leadership ultimately asks of us:

Not that we always know exactly where we are going.

Not that we never doubt ourselves.

But that we are willing, again and again, to listen closely enough to recognize when life is inviting us to become someone slightly braver, slightly more honest, and slightly more aligned with who we truly are.

If that invitation arrives quietly—through a moment of silence, uncertainty, or unexpected change—we should pay attention.

It might just be the sound of your real voice emerging.

After all, there are eight billion people in the world, and only one of them has your voice—so use it.

Simona Pappalardo

Simona Pappalardo is a leadership speaker, author, and former global executive who helps professionals navigate change with courage, clarity, and cultural intelligence. Drawing on a distinguished career in the electronics and manufacturing industry, she combines technical precision with a deeply human approach to leadership.

Having lived and worked across three continents, Simona brings a global perspective to conversations about authenticity, decision-making, and leading through complexity in today's rapidly changing world.

She is a sought-after speaker on modern leadership and has taken the stage at events including TEDWomen and the Military Influencer Conference. Through her speaking, writing, and coaching, she challenges leaders to move beyond titles and expectations and lead with clarity, conviction, and genuine connection. Her first book, *Authentically Yours: A Global Woman's Guide to Confident Leadership,* published in December 2025, quickly reached International Best-Seller status.

Connect with Simona

Website CoachingWithSimona.com

LinkedIn www.LinkedIn.com/in/SimonaPappalardo

Narratives That Define You

Joy Poli

External Labels

At some point in your life, you've had someone speak words about you that aren't true.

Too much.

Not enough.

Too emotional.

Not the right person.

What happens when you stop letting the words of others define you? You start living by standards that do.

I was often the last to leave the office—my job was to be there for the employees—even the ones who stayed late. That's the role of an HR Leader.

I remember rushing to the elevator on one of the few days I was able to leave "on time."

At the end of the day, the staff would pile into the elevator standing shoulder-to-should—everyone seemed to be competing to be the first one out. They were carrying their work shoes in their bag—wearing their gym shoes, ready to power walk.

Most of them lived in the city and relied on public transportation—specifically the train. They knew that a single minute could mean the difference between making it or standing outside in Chicago weather waiting.

And Chicago weather doesn't play around. The cold chills you to the bone. The rain seeps through your coat and shoes. The wind whips down the streets and against your face like the first slap of a fight. Snow sticks. This is why commuters plan their walk to and from the station with precision.

In Chicago, riding the train isn't casual.

It's commitment.

Miss your train, and you pay dearly.

I was determined to make the first elevator down—I had a one-year-old at home; that kind of urgency is primal.

As I sped down the hall, and rounded the corner, I heard it before I saw them:

"Shhhhh! HR is coming! The office police are here, shhhhh!!"

Laughter.

The elevator dinged. We all packed in like sardines. They're giggling, I smiled.

It stung.

I knew they didn't mean any harm. It was workplace banter.

But their behavior reinforced something I already knew. Something deeper.

HR rarely gets the glory—often looked at as "other" and not really part of the team.

Corporate Camouflage

I remember asking one day why sales staff that I sourced, helped recruit, and hire—the ones I saw the potential in, who were now surpassing goals and impressing higher-ups—were invited on the annual "Gold Club" trip, but I wasn't?

The office was a ghost town when they left.

Sales went.

Leadership went.

Not HR.

But I like fun in the sun! I am a sucker for all-inclusive.

But, because...

We weren't seen as revenue generators.

And because...

We were seen as the structure keepers.

Rule enforcers.

The constant.

We weren't invited to the celebration.

It didn't feel great. At all.

Sales could leave early when they hit their goals. There were games, prizes, and uncapped commissions. Celebration was built into their identity.

There was no equivalent for HR.

No scoreboard for retention.

No applause for navigating conflict quietly.

No reward for protecting the company from risk.

I understood the logic—I grew up in business, after all. I knew revenue drives business.

But I also knew something else:

It was about the people.

All of the people.

Culture drives sustainability.

And culture reveals itself in small moments:

In elevator jokes.

In who gets celebrated.

In who gets excluded.

Over time, the pattern became clear:

The jokes weren't random.

They echoed something.

They had been learned somewhere.

Somewhere along the way, HR had become the punchline.

It didn't start in the elevator.

It wasn't about the joke.

It was about perception.

And their perception told me everything I needed to know about the culture I was standing in—one that believed being unseen was part of being in HR.

The Awakening

I was told I had to be there.

And you may think I'm crazy saying this, but it was the last place I wanted to be.

It was a company-wide outing at a Cubs rooftop game. Loud. Packed. Everyone already in their cliques. Drinks in hand. The kind of event most people look forward to.

I didn't.

Baseball was never my thing. And I also wasn't sure how to show up in a setting like that. No one ever taught me how to be "social" in a room like this.

If I'm honest, I didn't know how to show up as anything other than HR.

So, conversations felt forced. I'd step into a group, smile and ask a few questions, respond to theirs. I laughed when everyone else laughed.

But none of it felt natural.

It felt performative.

Like I was showing up as a version of myself that didn't quite fit who I was—or who I wanted to become.

That's the part I was playing.

After years of being cast in a role I didn't want to be in:

The rule enforcer.

The structure keeper.

The office police.

When you spend years playing a "role" you never chose, you start to forget who you are outside of it.

I was performing the narrative that was handed to me, one I thought "came with the job."

Until one day I realized:

I didn't want to be less.

As Elyse Myers says, "If I'm too much, then go find less."

The Word

Years later, in a different work setting, I was given another label.

"Whiny."

I was working with a (former) Power Partner on a client search. He was using assessments to eliminate candidates instead of applying them to guide behavioral interview questions—which isn't HR best practice and goes against everything I was trained to do as a seasoned recruiter.

I was speaking as a trained subject matter expert in the field.

I wasn't emotional.

I wasn't being dramatic.

I was being passionate.

What frustrated me wasn't that he didn't know the best practices, it was that he wasn't advising according to them. His business model depended on more assessments being required—which inherently increases a candidate "fail rate." And in hiring, shortcuts like that have real consequences.

So, I pushed back.

He called me "whiny."

And, for a moment... I shut down.

Not because it was the first time I had been labeled, but because adulthood brings its own versions of those labels. The rooms are bigger. The stakes are higher. The language is more polished.

Later that week, after I took a beat and arranged my thoughts, I told him his word choice was wrong. He agreed and apologized. He told me his wife was a psychologist, and when he relayed the story to her, she explained how inappropriate it was to call a woman in business "whiny."

I accepted his apology.

But we never worked together again, because I had already made up my mind: My partners need to see me as an equal. If they don't, then we don't have a true partnership. I chose the high road, never mentioning it again.

A few years later, the client called me—the client who was *his* contact. They wanted to work with me again. They needed my expertise.

As we discussed their need, I asked if we'd be including my former Power Partner in the discussion. "No," said the client. "We're no longer working with him."

And that was it.

I never told the client what happened.

I didn't need to campaign.

I didn't smear.

I simply continued doing my work the way I always had.

Words spoken about you don't become fact.

You know who you are.

I knew who I was.

It was time I stopped hiding behind corporate camouflage.

That's where my real work began.

The Road That Led Me Here

If I'm honest, networking wasn't "new" to me, it just wasn't called networking.

I grew up in a family business. I watched how my parents operated. They held Visionary and Integrator roles. My mom focused on the backend and raising 5 children (and being pregnant 9 times). Needless to say, she had her hands full. My dad? He kept building. At one point, we had 5 retail bakeries and several wholesale bakeries. He was building so aggressively that he caught the attention of one of the biggest players in the industry and secured a contract as their only commercial bakery not owned by their parent company.

My dad has always been a risk taker. He's a pretty intense personality and as the driver of our family businesses, it never turned off.

I vividly remember being in Jamaica on a family vacation and my dad was chatting someone up (this was a regular occurrence—he has a likeable personality). When he came back to the family, I asked who that was and how he "knew" them. He said it was someone he worked with. It seemed like my dad always knew someone anywhere we went. Even in another country! He's one of the most gregarious people I've ever known, and he built his network in a very Chicago way. If you needed something, my dad's response was *always,* "I got a guy" (Chicago accent and all) and he'd make the introduction.

Need a mechanic? He's got a guy.

Need to remodel your business? He's got a guy.

Need something fixed, sourced, expedited, solved? He's got a guy.

He isn't transactional. He's relational.

Those referrals? They were built on trust. On history. On helping each other win.

That's how I thought business worked.

When Community Shows Up

My parents had more gut-wrenching moments in their business than any family should have to endure. At one point, their bakery burned down to the ground. Completely gone in the dark of the night.

My sister says she remembers watching it on the news. I was too young to remember it myself, but now, as a parent and business owner, I cannot imagine what they must have been going through. The fear. The uncertainty. The weight of knowing five kids depended on them to figure it out. And they didn't just have their kids to think of—what about their employees' families?

And then, something remarkable happened, in that moment.

Their community showed up.

People rallied around them—supporting them, encouraging them, and helping in ways that only a true community can.

Competitors opened their doors so my parents could continue to fulfill orders. Instead of going in for the kill and taking the opportunity for themselves, they offered their bakery space so my parents' staff could keep serving customers.

My father tells the story of how my godfather walked up to him, handed him a check, and walked away without saying a word. He said he never mentioned it again. My father has never shared the amount, but the way he tells the story, I know it was significant. It made a real difference in helping get my family back on our feet.

I absorbed that lesson without even realizing it:

Community is what carries you.

The part I didn't understand until much later was that their community didn't appear out of thin air.

It was built.

Nurtured.

Poured into over many years.

My mother had spent years doing that work. She spent endless hours with our church community—organizing, leading, and showing up for her inner circle again and again. She even went through the Deaconate Program alongside my father.

My dad got the title: **Deacon.**

My mom received a **Certificate of Completion.**

She's still a little salty about that—and rightfully so. She did the same work but received none of the recognition. Yet she kept giving to the community anyway: her time, her energy, and her care so that relationships could grow.

My dad was great at meeting people.

My mom was great at keeping them.

My dad's personality fills a room. It's helped him take risks, flex power, and build fast. But it also could sometimes fracture relationships. When that happened, my mom stepped in.

She repaired the cracks and kept the connection alive.

She handled the hard conversations and made sure the relationship remained intact.

And when the bakery burnt down, it was those relationships that carried our family through.

That's the community I grew up in.

That's how I saw business.

Which is why working in Corporate America later felt so jarring.

It felt foreign.

It felt pretend.

Because everything I knew about business growing up was real.

The lessons from my parents were imprinted on me.

But, somewhere between corporate titles and Cubs rooftops, networking became something else.

It became performative.

It became about optics.

More about who you were seen with than the impact you were making.

The networking I saw growing up wasn't loud.

It wasn't flashy.

It wasn't ego-driven (ok, maybe it was a bit; my dad has a healthy ego).

It was consistent.

Trust-based.

Natural.

That's when I realized something that changed everything...the problem wasn't that I was bad at networking. The problem was that I was practicing in rooms that defined it differently.

The Leap

After years in corporate HR, I knew many things weren't working for me anymore.

One of my biggest challenges was the expectation that HR always had to be there—never leaving early, coming in late, or calling off.

That reality was nearly impossible while pregnant and with a young child at home.

One day, during a panic attack, I called my sister Kim.

She said something that has stayed with me ever since: "Joy, **leap and the net will appear.**"

She had already done it—left teaching to build her own business so she could support her family and still be present in the moments that matter.

That call changed everything.

I put in my notice and soon after, I started my own HR Advisory firm: **Strategic Talent Resources.**

The Day the Rules Changed

I was driving home from a networking group I was paying a lot of money to be a part of—it was one of those groups that only allows one of each profession. One Attorney. One CPA. One marketing firm. And, one HR Advisory firm....or, at least that was the promise.

That day I walked into the meeting like I did every month, and sat down in my usual seat. Sitting across from me was a new nametag and company name. It was another HR Advisory firm.

I sat there stunned.

The leader casually said:

"You two will need to figure out where the line is so people know who to refer, and when."

I remember thinking, "You want *me* to find the line? I don't even know this guy—you brought him in. Didn't you think about this beforehand? I am your customer after all..."

How could he expect to ask the people I had spent years building trust with to suddenly split their loyalty?

It felt wrong. And I was pissed. Why didn't I matter to them?

So, I called my sister again.

The Birth of The Inner Circle

We started talking about all of the networking groups out there and the reasons that none of them felt right:

Too expensive.

Too restrictive.

Too transactional.

No ROI.

My sister mentioned that years earlier she had tried to build a group—it was a small one that jokingly called themselves the KAC (Kick @$$ Club) because she experienced the same frustrations I had in her various networking groups she paid to be in. Her main frustration was that she had been the top referrer in nearly every one of them, yet there wasn't much "get" to her "give"—because none of these people were ever taught how to open their networks to others. Or even why they should.

Networking had become transactional. So, she created a group she trusted. Her inner circle.

"Where's that group now?" I asked. She said something that stuck with me:

Communities need communication.

They need nurturing.

Being able to market them wasn't her issue. She was an award-winning marketer.

Keeping the community informed and all "rowing in the same direction" was.

Turns out, that's my strong suit—not that she would've known, as we hadn't worked together since I was about seven and she was fifteen.

"But I am good at that," I said.

And the rest is history. That is how The Inner Circle was born.

We had such uniquely different contacts that when put together, they complemented each other nicely.

We started with our people—our inner circle.

From there, their inner circles.

And so on.

I make it sound easy, but we relied heavily on my recruiting skills.

I could find anyone. Even your high school sweetheart. I was trained to be a "hunter" for the last 15 years. All I needed was the right messaging.

Kim knew how to build the brand. She was great at attracting new people. A real Pied Piper, if you will.

I knew how to build culture and foster relationship building.

Just like our parents, a true yin-and-yang moment.

VolunTOLD

When we started The Inner Circle, I wasn't thinking about becoming the authority in networking. I wanted to position myself at the top of a network to grow my business.

But something interesting started to happen. Members kept coming to me saying the same things:

"Why aren't the members buying from me?"

"I'm not getting value from the network."

"Why isn't anyone referring to me?"

Every conversation ended with me walking them through what we had built.

Eventually I called Kim again.

"I think we need a networking coach."

We tried bringing someone in.

It didn't work.

We tried again.

That didn't work either.

They were treating this like Sales 101 instead of meeting our members where they were in their business maturation.

Frustrated, I called Kim: "What now?"

"They already trust you. Maybe it's you."

Me?

I resisted.

Not because I am not ambitious.

Not because I didn't see the opportunity.

Because I didn't want to perform.

The thought literally brought me right back to that Cubs rooftop.

I didn't want to build out something new that would require me to perform.

But Kim had already seen what I couldn't see. Or, maybe I could, but I just needed to trust. To "leap and the net will appear."

My ability to connect people has never been accidental.

It's always been strategic.

It's always been something I take pride in.

She pushed me to own a title that had been looking for me for years:

Networking Coach.

We built rooms where relationships meant something.

Rooms where referrals were earned through trust.

Rooms where people could show up as their imperfect selves—as long as they were willing to grow!

Visibility came later.

Influence followed.

But the intention was *always* culture.

The Redefinition of Networking

Most people feel they *have* to network.

They don't *want* to.

They hate it.

I used to be one of them.

But what they actually hate isn't the networking:

It's the performing.

It's the feeling you get when you walk into a room and not a single person is willing to open their circle to make space for you.

The small talk feels like auditioning.

It's the subtle hierarchy of who matters, who doesn't.

The business cards shoved into hands.

The quantity over quality.

That isn't networking.

That's positioning.

Real networking isn't about visibility or proximity to power. It's a slow burn—it's deliberate work focused on building trust over time. It's about really listening to people's goals and truly understanding what matters to them. It's about showing up consistently. Relationships grow stronger over time.

Most people approach networking like an event: it has a starting line and a finish line. The best networkers know it's more than that. They know that if done right, your network can be a resource bench that makes you look good. Relationships don't appear in moments of need—they are built long before those moments arrive.

That's what a lot of people get wrong.

The networking I grew up with was very different.

My parents were happy producing for other brands behind the scenes. They didn't need the glitz and glamor of being the big name on the label. They didn't measure success by visibility. They measured it by relationships.

They taught me it wasn't about who you were seen with—it was about who stood beside you.

It wasn't about access.

It was about alignment.

It wasn't about collecting contacts.

It was about building trust.

Somewhere along the way, networking became something else:

It became flashy.

It was about optics and influence.

Thinking back, I realized what felt "off" to me on that rooftop wasn't because I was doing something wrong.

It wasn't my personality.

It was that I was trying to follow a script I had been handed—without understanding any of the context—instead of using what I was born with: the ability to read a room.

When I teach professionals how to network, I am not teaching them how to "work a room"; I teach them how to understand one.

The strongest networker isn't the loudest or flashiest.

They're the most perceptive.

They're strategic.

They see patterns.

They see the wall flowers.

They notice the overexposed.

They witness the awkward moments.

They recognize when trust is forming.

They sense when ego is eroding it.

It isn't magic.

It's architecture.

The way I teach networking is through six phases that happen simultaneously—much like a server in a restaurant managing different tables at different stages of the experience:

Exposure

Engagement

Trust

Collaboration

Retention

Expansion

Networking is not a funnel.

It's a responsibility.

Once you understand how relationships compound, you stop chasing proximity to power and you start to build ecosystems.

And, ecosystems are far more powerful than any flashy, fleeting moment.

Building What Didn't Exist

Redefining networking wasn't enough.

I had to build it differently.

When Kim and I started the Inner Circle, we made decisions —intentionally—that most networking organizations don't.

We curated.

Not to exclude, but to protect the culture.

We joke that we are the most inclusive, exclusive networking community.

But, it's true.

Not every room should be open to everyone. Not everyone should have access to everything.

Progression matters and should be considered.

Think about it—not every CEO wants to be contacted by every salesperson.

The finesse is all about timing: Timing in their business. Timing in their goals. Timing in a process.

We vet our members because every connection is meant to compound. If someone is only focused on the "get" and not the "give," it won't work.

We didn't structure our network around introductions.

We structured it around connections.

Collaborations.

Contributions.

And, support. Support in real moments:

When someone is battling cancer.

When someone's child needs help finding a job.

When someone is going through a divorce.

When someone needs someone to truly trust.

Our members are primed to respond.

Not as contacts.

As community.

Because titles don't lead.

Status doesn't dominate.

Contributions matter.

We encourage collaboration over competition.

Depth over volume.

Follow-up over flash.

In our community, the awards aren't given to the most polished. They're given to the most generous.

Generous with connections.

Generous with time.

Generous with care.

To the people who show up consistently—not just when it benefits them.

You don't need to have everything figured out to build a powerful network.

But you do need to be willing...

Willing to grow.

Willing to learn.

Willing to challenge yourself.

Willing to contribute.

Willing to reach down and help elevate someone else.

Because ecosystems don't thrive on ego.

They thrive on interconnection.

On collaboration.

On collective well-being.

They adapt to meet the needs of the whole.

That's where culture is built.

Not in the perfect elevator pitch.

But in consistent follow-through.

Where the network strengthens because people choose to strengthen it.

Intentionally.

By no longer working the room, but building within it.

The Spotlight

I did something I once believed I would never do.

I stood confidently in the spotlight.

It's not something I usually share beyond my close friends, but I have always had anxiety speaking on stage or in front of a group of people. Maybe because I learned as someone who was bullied as a child, that having all eyes on you isn't always a good thing.

Pair that with the reading disability I've had to work around my entire life—the one that made reading out loud feel like a threat instead of a skill—and you get a fear I carried quietly for years.

But The Inner Circle was never built for polished perfection.

It was built for people, like me, who were willing to show up as their authentically imperfect selves and challenge themselves to grow.

Kim knew that about me before I did.

Little by little, she challenged me to lead in new ways. It started with virtual introductions at events, and after many building blocks, I eventually moved to facilitating our virtual masterminds. From there, she ***volunTOLD*** me to speak at our in-person events. At first, I introduced speakers or presented awards. Eventually, I was giving my own talks.

She knew that if I wanted to build a culture rooted in connection, I would eventually have to be seen inside it.

And one day, I was.

I read my introduction out loud in a room of 150 professionals—a room we helped fill alongside our Power Partners.

Kim's voice cracked for a second as she introduced me. A proud big sister. My business coach. A full-circle moment.

When it was over, I didn't feel fearless. I felt relief. I felt accomplished. Not because the fear disappeared, but because I did it in spite of the fear. I didn't let the fear define me.

That's what being unmuted has come to mean for me:

Not louder.

Not flashier.

Willing to face it head-on.

Words spoken about you don't become fact, unless you let them. And the moment you stop performing and start participating—the moment you stop hiding and start showing up—your confidence not only grows.

It compounds.

Full Circle

Sometimes I think back to that elevator.

The whispers.

The laughter.

The version of me who smiled even though it stung.

I may be older now, but the feeling was the same. It pulled me right back into the fight-or-flight instinct I developed as a child trying to survive bullying at school.

Back then, I thought being unmuted meant proving myself.

Showing up how they wanted me to.

Fitting a mold.

Proving I belonged.

But, being unmuted isn't about proving.

It's about questioning:

Who decided performance was required for participation?

Who benefits when you shrink in rooms?

Who told you what networking should look like?

We all inherit narratives about who we should be—who we're allowed to be.

But what if the narrative isn't the truth?

What if it's the environment? Not you.

This time, I had a choice. I could shrink again or I could build differently.

The moment I stopped trying to be perfect was the moment I truly started.

Started designing my own space.

My own community.

Along the way, I've learned a lot about myself and about others.

Some view networking as "pay to play."

But a network isn't something you pay for; it's something you participate in.

We created a safe space to do the work—a space where others are doing it too.

A space to try.

To fail.

To learn.

To contribute.

To grow.

A space that thrives on participation—because the ecosystem doesn't work with or for passive members.

When you stop performing and start participating, you shift.

And when you shift, the room shifts.

And when the room shifts, what's possible inside it expands.

That's the work.

If you're ready to practice it—not just read about it—The Inner Circle is where participation replaces performance.

Where contribution matters most.

Where people grow together instead of compete for position.

And, for those of you who want to go deeper—who want to refine how they read rooms, connect, and lead intentionally inside professional spaces—that's the work I coach.

Because understanding connection is one thing.

Caring enough to do it differently—with intention and forethought—is another.

If you've never put real thought into your network, maybe it's time you do.

And if your network is truly working for you, then don't change a thing.

But if you've been performing to belong...

If you've been shrinking to fit...

Let this be your reminder:

Words spoken about you don't become fact.

Your standards do.

Joy Poli

Joy Poli is a master networker, relationship builder, and leadership connector who helps professionals elevate their influence and build powerful communities. As **Networking Coach for Accelerate Successfully**, Joy equips clients with the tools and mindset needed to create high-value, strategic relationships that fuel growth, opportunity, and long-term success.

Joy is also the **Co-Founder of The Inner Circle Network**, an exclusive professional community focused on business development, sales mastery, and leadership excellence. Through curated connections, dynamic training, and thought leadership platforms, Joy empowers members to grow their visibility and bottom line through authentic collaboration.

A true advocate for community-based leadership, Joy serves as **Chapter Leader of the Glenview/Northbrook Professional Moms**—a branch of the Professional Moms Community Network—supporting over 2,500 women balancing careers and family.

She leads both online and in-person gatherings, cultivating connection, mentorship, and support for professional moms at every stage.

In addition to her coaching and community-building roles, Joy is the **Owner of Strategic Talent Resources**, where she offers strategic HR advisory and recruiting solutions tailored to each business's unique needs. As a trusted **PEO Alternative**, Joy and her team help companies attract, hire, and retain top talent with a customized, hands-on approach.

Joy has fused her passions and professional expertise into one mission: helping others connect forward with clarity, purpose, and intention. Whether she's guiding clients through strategic networking or supporting business leaders with talent strategy, Joy brings heart, wisdom, and results to every relationship.

Connect with Joy

Accelerate Successfully

acceleratesuccessfully.com/coaching/network-coaching

Inner Circle oinnero.com

Strategic Talent Resources strategictalentresources.com

LinkedIn https://www.linkedin.com/in/joypoli

A Note from the Founders

Kim Kleeman and Joy Poli

Leadership isn't something that happens all at once. It is something that transforms people. When you step into your leadership role and use your own voice, opportunities to use it will come around. The Inner Circle creates those opportunities to find their voice and helps leaders hone that voice, find their purpose, and share it with the world. It's amazing to watch it happen!

These stories are just a few of our members who lead from within the Inner Circle Community. If this calls to you, then come check out an event to step into your leadership as well. Once you do so, you'll begin to build up other leaders who are empowered to lead and to grow a community to support their needs as well. We are watching it happen industry by industry, business by business, leader by leader and it is inspiring! When you choose to live unmuted, you create space for others to do the same. That's where real leadership begins.

YOUR TURN TO SPEAK!

Thank you for reading *Unmuted*. We hope that you've enjoyed this book and found it helpful. Please take a moment to use *your* voice and leave an honest review on Amazon and/or Goodreads. Please speak up and share your review with prospective readers. It's a great service you can offer to authors and the reading community.

Inner Circle Acknowledgements

Kim Kleeman

Thank you to so many wonderful people who contributed to this process. **The Inner Circle Press** was established in 2023 when we published the first book. In 2025, we expanded the team to better support our authors throughout their publishing journey, adding a writing mentor, editorial guidance, and marketing support to the process. A special thank-you to **Tami Palmer**, **Alina Rubin**, and **Becca Berkenstadt**, who have worked tirelessly to ensure each author feels supported and part of something truly special. They are amazing leaders who gave of themselves throughout this project—thank you!!

There's always remarkable team members who contribute to the process through their expertise such as **Wm. (Bill) Bullion** as our tireless proofreader. Funny story—Bill was one of my first freelancers I ever met and hired on one of my first-ever editorial projects. He's someone I admire and respect. **Danielle Epperson**, our marketing director, who helped design the cover and the Inner Circle Press and Lead from Within brands. Such beautiful rich work for us all! Thank you!

My partner in the Inner Circle, co-founder **Joy Poli** has managed the book process from the start, getting authors onboarded, working towards their goals, and writing her own chapter. Joy made sure this book got done, even amongst other great challenges. Watching Joy continue to grow and shine in her leadership has been an incredible gift. Thank you, Joy! Love you!

And of course those leaders who came before us—my parents, my brother Tom. They've given us advice and encouragement all along and paved the path before and alongside us.

I want to also personally thank my husband Jay, who grades his AP Math tests while I write these words. My partner, my motivator, my soulmate. He believes in every dream I bring to the table, and somehow helps make them possible, even if they seem impossible.

The Inner Circle community continues to impress me as it grows—leaders bringing ideas and integrating them, nurturing them and making them come to fruition. Cultivating this extraordinary group of leaders is one of the greatest privileges of my work.

We look forward to all the fruits of our labor in this book together. We are #Bettertogether.

Also by Inner Circle Press

Lead From Within: Entrepreneurs Share Proven Traits for Success

Unlock the Secrets to Success with Insights from Visionary Leaders

In *Lead From Within: Entrepreneurs Share Proven Traits for Success,* you'll embark on an extraordinary journey through the minds of accomplished leaders who have redefined the very essence of entrepreneurship. This thought-provoking anthology brings together a diverse group of trailblazers from various sectors, offering their invaluable wisdom and time-tested principles to guide you on your own path to success.

Drawing on the collective experiences of these visionary entrepreneurs, *Lead From Within* reveals the remarkable traits and strategies that set them apart. From technology innovators to social change agents, each contributor shares their unique insights into leadership, resilience, innovation, and more. You'll discover the common threads that unite these extraordinary individuals and the secrets behind their enduring success.

Available on Amazon

www.ingramcontent.com/pod-product-compliance
Lightning Source LLC
LaVergne TN
LVHW010948110826
845149LV00015B/3260

* 9 7 9 8 9 9 4 6 6 2 4 1 0 *